*Group's*

# BIBLESENSE™

 # GALATIANS

EXPERIENCING FREEDOM IN JESUS

# Group

Loveland, Colorado

www.group.com

# Group resources actually work!

This Group resource incorporates our R.E.A.L. approach to ministry. It reinforces a growing friendship with Jesus, encourages long-term learning, and results in life transformation, because it's

**Relational**
Leaner-to-learner interaction enhances learning and builds Christian friendships.

**Experiential**
What learners experience through discussion and action sticks with them up to 9 times longer than what they simply hear or read.

**Applicable**
The aim of Chistian education is to equip learners to be both hearers and doers of God's Word.

**Learner-based**
Learners understand and retain more when the learning process takes into consideration how they learn best.

## *Group's* BIBLESENSE™

**GALATIANS:** Experiencing Freedom in Jesus
Copyright © 2007 Group Publishing, Inc.

Visit our Web site: **www.group.com**

## Credits
Contributors: Jonathan Boggs, Joy-Elizabeth F. Lawrence, Keith Madsen, Jeff White, and Roxanne Wieman
Editor: Carl Simmons
Creative Development Editor: Matt Lockhart
Chief Creative Officer: Joani Schultz
Copy Editor: Alison Imbriaco
Design and Production Contributors: Jean Bruns, Joyce Douglas, Kari Monson, Kevin Mullins, Jeff Storm,
     Andrea Filer, Anne Wilseck
Photographer: Randy Pfizenmaier, FUSEBOX studio
Production Manager: DeAnne Lear

Unless otherwise indicated, all Scripture quotations are taken from the *Holy Bible*, New Living Translation, copyright © 1996, 2004. Used by permission of Tyndale House Publishers, Inc., Wheaton, Illinois 60189. All rights reserved.

**Library of Congress Cataloging-in-Publication Data**
Galatians : experiencing freedom in Jesus.
     p.  cm. -- (Group's BibleSense)
Includes bibliographical references.
ISBN-13: 978-0-7644-3244-6 (pbk. : alk. paper)
1. Bible. N.T. Galatians--Textbooks.  2. Bible, N.T. Galatians--Criticism,
interpretation, etc.   I. Group Publishing.
  BS2685.55.G35  2006
  227' .40071--dc22
                        2006024672

10 9 8 7 6 5 4 3 2 1     16 15 14 13 12 11 10 09 08 07
Printed in the United States of America.

# CONTENTS

# CONTENTS CONTINUED

# INTRODUCTION

## TO GROUP'S BIBLESENSE™

**W**elcome to **Group's BibleSense**™, a book-of-the-Bible series unlike any you've ever seen! This is a Bible study series in which you'll literally be able to *See, Hear, Smell, Taste, and Touch God's Word*—not only through seeing and hearing the actual book of the Bible you're studying on DVD, but also through thought-provoking questions and group activities. As you do these sessions, you'll bring the Word to life, bring your group closer together as a community, and help your group members bring that life to others.

Whether you're new to small groups or have been doing them for years, you'll discover new, exciting, and—dare we say it—*fun* ways to learn and apply God's Word to your life. And as you dig deeper into the Bible passage for each session and its meaning for your life, you'll find your life (and the lives around you) transformed more and more into Jesus' likeness.

Each session concludes with a series of opportunities on how to commit to reaching your world with the Bible passage you've just studied—whether it's changing your own responses to others, reaching out to them individually or as an entire group, or by taking part in something bigger than your group.

So again, welcome to the world of BibleSense! We hope that you'll find the experiences and studies here both meaningful and memorable and that as you do them together, your lives will grow even more into the likeness of our Lord, Jesus Christ.

—*Carl Simmons, Editor*

# ABOUT THE SESSIONS

## TASTE AND SEE (20 minutes)

Every BibleSense session begins with food—to give you a chance to unwind and transition from a busy day and other preoccupations into the theme of the session. After the food and a few introductory questions, you'll get to experience Scripture in a fresh way. The passage for each session is included on DVD, as well as in print within the book. Also provided is "A Sense of History," a brief feature offering additional cultural and historical context.

## DIGGING INTO SCRIPTURE (30 minutes)

This is the central part of the session. You'll have the chance to interact with the Scripture passage you've just read and watched, and, through questions and other sensory experiences, you'll learn how it applies to *your* life.

## MAKING IT PERSONAL (15 minutes)

Now you'll move from understanding *how* the passage applies to your life, to thinking about ways you *can* apply it. In this part of the session, meaningful experiences and questions bring personal meaning home.

## TOUCHING YOUR WORLD (25 minutes)

This is the "take home" part of the session. You'll choose a weekly challenge to directly apply this session's passage in a practical way in the week ahead, as well as share prayer requests and pray for one another. Also included is a "Taking It Home" section, with tips on how you can prepare for your next session.

# GETTING CONNECTED

Pass your books around the room, and have group members write in their names, phone numbers, e-mail addresses, and birthdays.

| Name | Phone | E-mail | Birthday |
| --- | --- | --- | --- |
| | | | |
| | | | |
| | | | |
| | | | |
| | | | |
| | | | |
| | | | |
| | | | |
| | | | |
| | | | |

# SESSION 1:

# KEEPING IT REAL

GALATIANS 1:1-24

In this session, you'll discover how to tell between real freedom in Jesus and things that promise freedom without Jesus.

## PRE-SESSION CHECKLIST:

☐ **Leader:** Check out the Session 1 Leader Notes in the back of the book (page 91).

☐ **Food Coordinator:** If you are responsible for the Session 1 snack, see page 102.

☐ **Supplies:**
- 1 popular magazine for each subgroup
- 1 index card for each person in the group (optional)

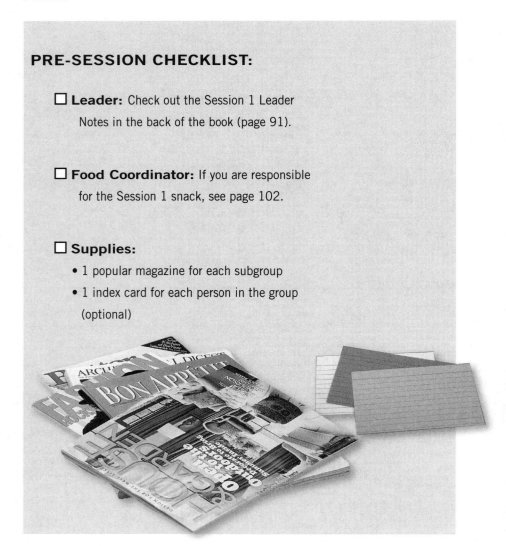

# *TASTE AND SEE* (20 minutes)

There are two sets of bowls of ice cream set out. Following your Food Coordinator's directions, grab a bowl from the first set and enjoy. Find a partner—someone you don't know very well— and take a few minutes to share some things about yourself while you're eating. Then share your answers to the following questions:

- What's one of your favorite books of fiction? What do you like about it?

- OK, so what's one of your favorite *nonfiction* books? What do you like about *that*? How are the things you like about each book different?

*If this is your first time together as a group, pass your books around to record each other's contact information (page 7), either at the start or end of this session.*

Gather together as a large group. Take turns introducing your partner to the group.

Now, go ahead and take another bowl of ice cream, this time from the other set. As you enjoy this bowl, discuss the following:

- How were the two bowls of ice cream different?

- Which one did you prefer, and why?

 Watch the first chapter on the DVD (Galatians 1:1-24). This passage can also be found on the following page if you would like to follow along in your book.

## Galatians 1:1-24 (NLT)

[1]This letter is from Paul, an apostle. I was not appointed by any group of people or any human authority, but by Jesus Christ himself and by God the Father, who raised Jesus from the dead.

[2]All the brothers and sisters here join me in sending this letter to the churches of Galatia.

[3]May God our Father and the Lord Jesus Christ give you grace and peace. [4]Jesus gave his life for our sins, just as God our Father planned, in order to rescue us from this evil world in which we live. [5]All glory to God forever and ever! Amen.

[6]I am shocked that you are turning away so soon from God, who called you to himself through the loving mercy of Christ. You are following a different way that pretends to be the Good News [7]but is not the Good News at all. You are being fooled by those who deliberately twist the truth concerning Christ.

[8]Let God's curse fall on anyone, including us or even an angel from heaven, who preaches a different kind of Good News other than the one we preached to you. [9]I say again what we have said before: If anyone preaches any other Good News than the one you welcomed, let that person be cursed.

[10]Obviously, I'm not trying to win the approval of people, but of God. If pleasing people were my goal, I would not be Christ's servant.

[11]Dear brothers and sisters, I want you to understand that the gospel message I preach is not based on mere human reasoning. [12]I received my message from no human source, and no one taught me. Instead, I received it by direct revelation from Jesus Christ.

¹³You know what I was like when I followed the Jewish religion—how I violently persecuted God's church. I did my best to destroy it. ¹⁴I was far ahead of my fellow Jews in my zeal for the traditions of my ancestors.

¹⁵But even before I was born, God chose me and called me by his marvelous grace. Then it pleased him ¹⁶to reveal his Son to me so that I would proclaim the Good News about Jesus to the Gentiles.

When this happened, I did not rush out to consult with any human being. ¹⁷Nor did I go up to Jerusalem to consult with those who were apostles before I was. Instead, I went away into Arabia, and later I returned to the city of Damascus.

¹⁸Then three years later I went to Jerusalem to get to know Peter, and I stayed with him for fifteen days. ¹⁹The only other apostle I met at that time was James, the Lord's brother. ²⁰I declare before God that what I am writing to you is not a lie.

²¹After that visit I went north into the provinces of Syria and Cilicia. ²²And still the Christians in the churches in Judea didn't know me personally. ²³All they knew was that people were saying, "The one who used to persecute us is now preaching the very faith he tried to destroy!" ²⁴And they praised God because of me.

# DIGGING INTO SCRIPTURE (30 minutes)

**Tip:** To maximize participation and to be sure you'll have enough time to work through each session, we recommend breaking into smaller subgroups of three or four at various points.

As a group, discuss:

• What thoughts or emotions came to your mind as you watched this session's Bible passage?

Read Galatians 1:6-10 and the "A Sense of History" feature directly below. Then discuss the questions that follow.

## A SENSE OF HISTORY

### Setting the Record Straight

The region of Galatia was located in what is now Turkey. Paul passed through the cities of Galatia during his first three missionary journeys and wrote this letter to the churches there sometime between 49 A.D. and 56 A.D. He felt this message was so important that he wrote it with his own hand, instead of following his regular practice of dictating to a secretary.

The apostle Paul played a very unusual role in early Christian history. While the other "pillars of the church" (including the apostles Peter, James, and John) were preaching the gospel to the Jews, Paul had been called by God to bring the message of Jesus to the Gentiles (non-Jews).

However, Paul faced a growing challenge from some of his fellow Christian leaders, especially those in the churches of Galatia. He heard that many of the Jewish-raised leaders were requiring Christians (both Jews and Gentiles) to adhere to the old laws of Judaism—the original laws from the time of Moses—rather than embrace their freedom in Jesus. These "Judaizers" were essentially requiring "faith by works" and Paul wanted nothing to do with it. Therefore, he wrote this letter as a point-by-point case defending "faith by grace."

• Put yourself in the place of the church leaders in Galatia. Why might you be tempted to stick to the old laws? What reasons does Paul give here?

• What special challenges do you think the Galatians might have faced in order to change their old ways of thinking and follow Jesus instead?

Now, break into subgroups.

**Leader:** Give each subgroup one magazine of its choice.

**Subgroup Leaders:** Use a maximum of 15 minutes for your discussion time.

Flip through the magazine together. Choose one advertisement that your subgroup agrees would appeal to readers, and then discuss the following:

• What exaggerations or false suggestions do you see in this ad? Why do you think those things are included here?

• If you could redo this ad, what would you say or show to make its promises more accurate?

"Then Jesus said, 'Come to me, all you who are weary and carry heavy burdens, and I will give you rest. Take my yoke upon you. Let me teach you, because I am humble and gentle at heart, and you will find rest for your souls. For my yoke is easy to bear, and the burden I give you is light'."
—Matthew 11:28-30

• Now, think about a time you felt God had really given you a specific promise or direction for your life and you obeyed him. How did others react—and what suggestions did they have—as you obeyed God? How did you respond to those reactions or suggestions?

• In what ways did you experience God's freedom during that time?

Come together as a larger group, and share any highlights or questions from your subgroup discussion.

# *MAKING IT PERSONAL* (15 minutes)

Read Galatians 1:13-24, and then discuss these questions:

• What changes do you see here in Paul's understanding of who God is and what God really wants?

• In what ways have you experienced the freedom of Jesus in your own life? How have those experiences changed your own understanding of who God is and what he wants?

• Where do you still need God to change your perspective right now? What's one thing you can do to remember the freedom you have in Jesus and apply regularly to your life?

> **Think about it!**
> President Franklin D. Roosevelt said, "Freedom of speech is of no use to a man who has nothing to say and freedom of worship is of no use to a man who has lost his God."

# *TOUCHING YOUR WORLD* (25 minutes)

Review the following "weekly challenge" options, and select the challenge you'd like to do. Turn to a partner, and share your choice. Then make plans to connect with your partner sometime between now and the next session to check in with and encourage one another.

☐ **DECIDE WHAT SIDE YOU'RE ON.** Get an index card from your Session Leader. On one side, complete the following sentence: "One lie about me that I find easy to believe is…" On the other side, complete this sentence: "One truth about me I find hard to believe is…" Commit to praying with your partner now and during the week that you'll be able to distinguish the truth from the lies in your life and that you will be able to use God's truth to counter the lies in your life.

☐ **SEE THE JESUS IN YOU THAT OTHERS SEE.** Contact three trusted people you are or have been close to (such as parents, teachers, supervisors, or old friends). Ask these people what things they like best about you, and keep a list. Then read ahead in Galatians 5:22-23 to see God's definition of the fruit of the Spirit, and compare that list to the list of what others see in you. Discover the truth about the fruitfulness of your spiritual journey so far, and take time to thank God for it.

☐ **THE TRUTH *ISN'T* "OUT THERE."** Find a book or Web site that reveals the truth about a specific cult or Christian fringe group. Think about how Paul would address the group's take on the good news of Jesus. Does the group preach a message of freedom and grace? Commit to having an open and honest discussion with someone from one of these groups—or with a non-Christian friend—about the real meaning of freedom in Christ.

Come together as a group. Share prayer requests. Before the leader prays, take a few moments to be silent and appreciate God's grace in your life.

**Leader:** If you haven't already, take a few minutes to review the group roles and assignments (pages 99-101) with the group. At minimum, be sure that the food and supplies responsibilities for the next session are covered.

## Until next time...

Date _____

Time _____

Place _____

## Taking It Home:

**1.** Set a goal for how many times you'll either read through or watch on your DVD the Session 2 Bible passage (Galatians 2:1-21). Make a point to read the "A Sense of History" feature in Session 2 (page 22) before the next session. You may also want to review this week's passage as well. Let your weekly challenge partner know what goals you've set so he or she can encourage you and help hold you accountable.

**2.** Touch base sometime before the next session with your weekly challenge partner to compare notes on how you're both doing with the goals you've set.

**3.** If you have volunteered for a role or signed up to help with food or supplies for the next session, be sure to prepare. The Session 2 supplies list can be found on page 18, and the Food Coordinator instructions are on page 102.

**4. I commit to touching my world this week by discovering and sharing the freedom of Jesus in the following ways:**

_____

_____

_____

# SESSION 2:

# FREEDOM IS...
# FREE

**In this session, you'll learn how to better live out your freedom in Jesus.**

## PRE-SESSION CHECKLIST:

☐ **Leader:** Check out the Session 2 Leader Notes in the back of the book (page 92).

☐ **Food Coordinator:** If you are responsible for the Session 2 snack, see page 102.

☐ **Supplies:**
  • None

# *TASTE AND SEE* (20 minutes)

There are a variety of cereals for you to enjoy this session. But first, break into pairs, and share your answers to the following:

- What was your favorite cereal as a kid?

- What do you usually eat for breakfast now?

After sharing, your pair should come up with one rule that everyone will need to follow to eat the cereal. Be as simple or creative as you like. For example, one rule might be that everyone has to eat the cereal with his or her left hand. Another might be that everyone has to chew each bite exactly 15 times.

Take two or three minutes to come up with your rule. Then grab a bowl of cereal, and come together as a large group. Share your pair's rule, and then demonstrate it with your cereal (as best you can). Try everyone else's rules with your cereal, too.

Afterward, discuss the following:

- Which of these rules helped you enjoy your cereal? Which ones didn't? Why (in both cases)?

Hang onto your spoons. You'll need them again in a little while.

Watch the second chapter on the DVD (Galatians 2:1-21). This passage can also be found on the following page if you would like to follow along in your book.

> **Did you know?** The first breakfast cereal was invented by James Jackson in Danville, New York, in 1863. Called Granula, it offered high-fiber relief from the greasy eggs-and-meat breakfasts of the day. It never became popular, though, because the heavy bran nuggets were too hard to eat unless they were soaked overnight.

# Galatians 2:1-21 (NLT)

¹Then fourteen years later I went back to Jerusalem again, this time with Barnabas; and Titus came along, too. ²I went there because God revealed to me that I should go. While I was there I met privately with those considered to be leaders of the church and shared with them the message I had been preaching to the Gentiles. I wanted to make sure that we were in agreement, for fear that all my efforts had been wasted and I was running the race for nothing. ³And they supported me and did not even demand that my companion Titus be circumcised, though he was a Gentile.

⁴Even that question came up only because of some so-called Christians there—false ones, really—who were secretly brought in. They sneaked in to spy on us and take away the freedom we have in Christ Jesus. They wanted to enslave us and force us to follow their Jewish regulations. ⁵But we refused to give in to them for a single moment. We wanted to preserve the truth of the gospel message for you.

⁶And the leaders of the church had nothing to add to what I was preaching. (By the way, their reputation as great leaders made no difference to me, for God has no favorites.) ⁷Instead, they saw that God had given me the responsibility of preaching the gospel to the Gentiles, just as he had given Peter the responsibility of preaching to the Jews. ⁸For the same God who worked through Peter as the apostle to the Jews also worked through me as the apostle to the Gentiles.

⁹In fact, James, Peter, and John, who were known as pillars of the church, recognized the gift God had given me, and they accepted Barnabas and me as their co-workers. They encouraged us to keep preaching to the Gentiles, while they continued their work with the Jews. ¹⁰Their only suggestion was that we keep on helping the poor, which I have always been eager to do.

¹¹But when Peter came to Antioch, I had to oppose him to his face, for what he did was very wrong. ¹²When he first arrived, he ate with the

Gentile Christians, who were not circumcised. But afterward, when some friends of James came, Peter wouldn't eat with the Gentiles anymore. He was afraid of criticism from these people who insisted on the necessity of circumcision. ¹³As a result, other Jewish Christians followed Peter's hypocrisy, and even Barnabas was led astray by their hypocrisy.

¹⁴When I saw that they were not following the truth of the gospel message, I said to Peter in front of all the others, "Since you, a Jew by birth, have discarded the Jewish laws and are living like a Gentile, why are you now trying to make these Gentiles follow the Jewish traditions?

¹⁵ "You and I are Jews by birth, not 'sinners' like the Gentiles. ¹⁶Yet we know that a person is made right with God by faith in Jesus Christ, not by obeying the law. And we have believed in Christ Jesus, so that we might be made right with God because of our faith in Christ, not because we have obeyed the law. For no one will ever be made right with God by obeying the law."

¹⁷But suppose we seek to be made right with God through faith in Christ and then we are found guilty because we have abandoned the law? Would that mean Christ has led us into sin? Absolutely not! ¹⁸Rather, I am a sinner if I rebuild the old system of law I already tore down. ¹⁹For when I tried to keep the law, it condemned me. So I died to the law—I stopped trying to meet all its requirements—so that I might live for God. ²⁰My old self has been crucified with Christ. It is no longer I who live, but Christ lives in me. So I live in this earthly body by trusting in the Son of God, who loved me and gave himself for me. ²¹I do not treat the grace of God as meaningless. For if keeping the law could make us right with God, then there was no need for Christ to die.

# A SENSE OF HISTORY
## Paul Plants the Seeds

When people think about Paul, various roles come to mind: apostle, preacher, leader, author, and martyr. But perhaps his most important calling was as a missionary. Paul said that God himself had "given me the responsibility of preaching the gospel to the Gentiles" (verse 7), and he spent the remainder of his life fulfilling that calling.

Over the course of 20 years, Paul went on three missionary journeys in the northern Mediterranean area, through the Middle East, and into Europe. His first trip, starting about 16 years after Jesus died, followed the main trade routes through what is now known as Syria, Turkey, and Greece. Paul never traveled alone—Luke was one of his most constant companions, and he recorded Paul's journeys in great detail in the book of Acts.

Upon arriving in a new city, Paul would preach in synagogues and other public places, usually to large groups of people. He would then build relationships with new converts and help start local churches. Paul personally founded the early churches in the area of Galatia during his first missionary journey and then visited many of those churches during his second and third missionary journeys.

Once Paul moved on to a new city, he trusted the local church leaders to carry the torch of the gospel message. He wrote many letters to provide teaching and encouragement to the churches he started. But when news reached him that some in the churches in Galatia were distorting that message, he wrote this letter to set the record straight.

# DIGGING INTO SCRIPTURE (30 minutes)

As a group, discuss:

• What thoughts or emotions came to your mind as you watched this session's Bible passage?

Now break into subgroups.

**Leader:** Give each subgroup a box of cereal, and make sure every subgroup member still has a spoon.

**Subgroup Leaders:** Use no more than 20 minutes for your discussion time.

In your subgroup, discuss the following:

• What are some rules you had to follow as a kid that you no longer need to follow? Why don't you have to follow those rules anymore?

Pile as many pieces of cereal on your spoon as you can. Then try to pass the spoons around your subgroup without dropping any of the cereal. See if you can pass the spoons around the entire subgroup at least once before the cereal spills.

Afterward, read Galatians 2:17-21, and discuss the following questions:

• How determined were you to keep your cereal from spilling? What thoughts came to mind as you were either receiving or passing along your spoonful?

• How wrapped up do you get in doing things "just right"? How was this activity similar to that? How was it different?

• When have you tried to gain God's favor by "doing" things "for him"? What was the result?

**Think about it:**

*Thomas Edison once said: "There are no rules here—we're trying to accomplish something." What rules do you need to re-examine through God's eyes so that you can accomplish what God really wants for your life?*

• On a scale of 1 to 10, how hard is it for you to trust Jesus when things around you aren't going the way you think they should (1 being "I'll take care of it," 10 being "I know Jesus always wants the best for me, even if I don't understand it")? Explain.

• What are some ways you've seen yourself (or others) changed by Jesus as you've trusted different areas of your life to him rather than trying to do it on your own?

Come together as a larger group, and share any highlights or questions from your subgroup discussion.

# MAKING IT PERSONAL (15 minutes)

Read Galatians 2:11-16, and then discuss the following questions:

• What do you think was going through Peter's head before, during, and after this incident? How about Paul?

• Which of the two men in this situation is more like you? Why?

• Read Matthew 16:17-19 in the margin. How do you explain Peter's behavior in this passage of Galatians—which takes place years after Jesus gave Peter his name?

• In what situations do you still tend to back away from trusting God, despite having seen God's goodness and promises? What's one step you can take right now to exercise your freedom in Jesus in that situation?

> "Jesus replied, 'You are blessed, Simon son of John, because my Father in heaven has revealed this to you. You did not learn this from any human being. Now I say to you that you are Peter (which means "rock") and upon this rock I will build my church, and all the powers of hell will not conquer it. And I will give you the keys of the Kingdom of Heaven. Whatever you forbid on earth will be forbidden in heaven, and whatever you permit on earth will be permitted in heaven.' "
> —Matthew 16:17-19

# *TOUCHING YOUR WORLD* (25 minutes)

Review the following "weekly challenge" options, and select the challenge you'd like to do. Turn to a partner, and share your choice. Then make plans to connect with your partner sometime between now and the next session to check in with and encourage one another.

☐ **BREAK YOUR OWN RULES.** Take a few minutes to list all the "rules" you impose on your faith. Do you have personal rituals or traditions or things you feel obligated to do? Pick one day this week to break one or all of those rules that really aren't God-given and concentrate only on your freedom in Christ. At the end of the day, reflect on the thoughts and emotions you experienced as you relied on God rather on your own rules—and what you might do differently in the future as a result.

☐ **MAKE A LIST, AND CHECK IT ONCE.** Draw two columns on a sheet of paper. In one column, list all the things in life you have to pay for. In the other column, list all the things in life that are free. Look over your two lists, and compare and contrast the value of each one. Which things do you need? Which things could you live without? Then put a checkmark next to all the things (free or not) that God provides for you. Thank God for each of them.

☐ **CAM ON THE STREET.** Grab a video camera, and interview approximately 10 people (preferably strangers) about their thoughts on rules and freedom. Ask them three questions: 1) "Do you think rules are necessary? Why or why not?" 2) "What does 'freedom' mean to you?" 3) "Can a person be truly free while being subject to a bunch of rules?" Once your interviews are done, get together with two or three friends (or your small group), watch your video, and talk about what the responses reveal about faith in Jesus.

☐ **GO DIRECTLY TO JAIL.** Visit a local jail or prison, and talk to the chaplain about what life is like in an isolated cell. If possible, interview an inmate about his or her experience on the inside. Pray with him or her. Then prayerfully consider the realities of freedom versus slavery in your spiritual life.

Come together as a group. Share prayer requests. Before starting prayer, take a few moments to be silent and appreciate the freedom God has given you.

## Until next time...

Date _____

Time _____

Place _____

## Taking It Home:

1. Set a goal for how many times you'll either read through or watch on your DVD the Session 3 Bible passage (Galatians 3:1-25). Make a point to read the "A Sense of History" feature in Session 3 (page 32) before the next session. You may also want to review this week's passage as well. Let your weekly challenge partner know what goals you've set so he or she can encourage you and help hold you accountable.

2. Touch base sometime before the next session with your weekly challenge partner to compare notes on how you're both doing with the goals you've set.

3. If you have volunteered for a role or signed up to help with food or supplies for the next session, be sure to prepare for this. The Session 3 supplies list can be found on page 28, and the Food Coordinator instructions are on page 103.

4. **I commit to touching my world this week by living out my freedom in Jesus in the following ways:**

_____

_____

_____

_____

_____

# SESSION 3:

## DON'T DO IT YOURSELF!

GALATIANS 3:1-25

In this session, you'll further examine how to rely more on God's grace and how to share it with others.

## PRE-SESSION CHECKLIST:

☐ **Leader:** Check out the Session 3 Leader Notes in the back of the book (page 93).

☐ **Food Coordinator:** If you are responsible for the Session 3 snack, see page 103.

☐ **Supplies:**

- 2 identical pictures per subgroup

- 1 roll of tape per subgroup

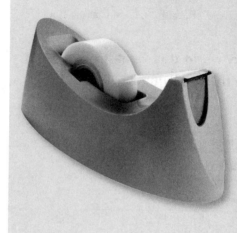

# TASTE AND SEE (20 minutes)

Go ahead and choose your favorite kind of chocolate. Then take some time to *really* enjoy it. Close your eyes. Let it roll around in your mouth. Really *savor* the taste.

After you've had a chance to enjoy your chocolate, discuss the following questions:

• What words would you use to describe the taste of chocolate?

• Which of those same words could you use to describe God's gift of grace (or God's goodness)? Explain the words you chose.

• In what ways is God's grace *not* like chocolate?

Watch the third chapter on the DVD (Galatians 3:1-25).

# Galatians 3:1-25 (NLT)

[1]Oh, foolish Galatians! Who has cast an evil spell on you? For the meaning of Jesus Christ's death was made as clear to you as if you had seen a picture of his death on the cross. [2]Let me ask you this one question: Did you receive the Holy Spirit by obeying the law of Moses? Of course not! You received the Spirit because you believed the message you heard about Christ. [3]How foolish can you be? After starting your Christian lives in the Spirit, why are you now trying to become perfect by your own human effort? [4]Have you experienced so much for nothing? Surely it was not in vain, was it?

[5]I ask you again, does God give you the Holy Spirit and work miracles among you because you obey the law? Of course not! It is because you believe the message you heard about Christ.

[6]In the same way, "Abraham believed God, and God counted him as righteous because of his faith." [7]The real children of Abraham, then, are those who put their faith in God.

[8]What's more, the Scriptures looked forward to this time when God would declare the Gentiles to be righteous because of their faith. God proclaimed this good news to Abraham long ago when he said, "All nations will be blessed through you." [9]So all who put their faith in Christ share the same blessing Abraham received because of his faith.

[10]But those who depend on the law to make them right with God are under his curse, for the Scriptures say, "Cursed is everyone who does not observe and obey all the commands that are written in God's Book of the Law." [11]So it is clear that no one can be made right with God by trying to keep the law. For the Scriptures say, "It is through faith that a righteous person has life." [12]This way of faith is very different from the way of law, which says, "It is through obeying the law that a person has life."

[13]But Christ has rescued us from the curse pronounced by the law. When he was hung on the cross, he took upon himself the curse for our wrongdoing. For it is written in the Scriptures, "Cursed is everyone who is hung on a tree." [14]Through Christ Jesus, God has blessed the Gentiles with the same blessing he promised to Abraham, so that we who are believers might receive the promised Holy Spirit through faith.

¹⁵Dear brothers and sisters, here's an example from everyday life. Just as no one can set aside or amend an irrevocable agreement, so it is in this case. ¹⁶God gave the promises to Abraham and his child. And notice that the Scripture doesn't say "to his children," as if it meant many descendants. Rather, it says "to his child"—and that, of course, means Christ. ¹⁷This is what I am trying to say: The agreement God made with Abraham could not be canceled 430 years later when God gave the law to Moses. God would be breaking his promise. ¹⁸For if the inheritance could be received by keeping the law, then it would not be the result of accepting God's promise. But God graciously gave it to Abraham as a promise.

¹⁹Why, then, was the law given? It was given alongside the promise to show people their sins. But the law was designed to last only until the coming of the child who was promised. God gave his law through angels to Moses, who was the mediator between God and the people. ²⁰Now a mediator is helpful if more than one party must reach an agreement. But God, who is one, did not use a mediator when he gave his promise to Abraham.

²¹Is there a conflict, then, between God's law and God's promises? Absolutely not! If the law could give us new life, we could be made right with God by obeying it. ²²But the Scriptures declare that we are all prisoners of sin, so we receive God's promise of freedom only by believing in Jesus Christ.

²³Before the way of faith in Christ was available to us, we were placed under guard by the law. We were kept in protective custody, so to speak, until the way of faith was revealed.

²⁴Let me put it another way. The law was our guardian until Christ came; it protected us until we could be made right with God through faith. ²⁵And now that the way of faith has come, we no longer need the law as our guardian.

# A SENSE OF HISTORY

## It's the Law...or Is It?

Throughout the New Testament, there's evidence that Jewish Christians were attempting to force their Gentile brothers and sisters to follow the code of the Mosaic Law (check out Acts 15, Romans 2, Ephesians 2–3, and Colossians 2). And throughout the New Testament, Paul argues against this, reminding the Jewish Christians that they are no longer under Jewish Law and should not expect the Gentile Christians to be enslaved by that same law.

The Mosaic Law's 613 commands include 365 negative and 248 positive commands. These rules guide every aspect of life: moral, social, and ceremonial.

The moral law (the Ten Commandments) instructs people about principles of right and wrong. Social commandments, or judgments, instruct people in secular, political, and economic affairs. The ordinances, or ceremonial law, instructs Israel in worship and spiritual practices. These rules also govern the priesthood, the tabernacle (the Jewish holy place that contained relics of their faith), and sacrifices.

Paul argues again and again that Christians are to live righteously by a new law: Jesus Christ. Through the indwelling of the Holy Spirit and the manifestation of God's grace, Christians are instructed and trained in how to live a life that pleases God.

As a group, discuss:

• What thoughts or emotions came to your mind as you watched this session's Bible passage, whether just now or during the past week?

Now break into subgroups.

**Leader:** Give each subgroup leader two identical pictures and one roll of tape.

**Subgroup Leaders:** Use a maximum of 20 minutes for your discussion time.

Pass one of the pictures around your subgroup. Each person should hold the picture, say one sin that he or she has done, and then tear off a piece of the picture. Be sure to keep all the pieces.

When everyone has taken a turn, discuss the following:

• What things came to mind as you tore the picture?

As a subgroup, use the tape to put the pieces of your picture back together. Then read Galatians 3:9-14, and discuss the following questions:

• Describe a time you felt like sin was tearing up your life. What things did you do to try to put your life back together?

• What things do you remember God doing to help restore you during that time? In what ways was what God did different from your own efforts?

Now, compare your intact picture with the taped-up picture, and discuss the following:

"For everyone has sinned; we all fall short of God's glorious standard."
—Romans 3:23

• Read the quote from Romans in the margin. If every person has sinned and fallen short of God's standard, then everyone's life is like our torn-up picture. How is the untorn picture a metaphor for God's grace? How is it different?

"The world runs by ungrace. Everything depends on what I do...Jesus' kingdom calls us to another way, one that depends not on our performance but his own. We do not have to achieve but merely follow. He has already earned for us the costly victory of God's acceptance."
—Philip Yancey, What's So Amazing About Grace?

• How did you react the first time you heard that we're saved by the grace of God? In what ways has that idea become real to you since then?

• Where in your life do you still need to see God's grace more clearly? What might help you to do that?

Come together as a large group, and share any highlights or questions from your subgroup discussion.

# *MAKING IT PERSONAL* (15 minutes)

> *"I think I'll go to heaven because I've always tried to be a good person."*

Read the quote above.

• Have you ever heard anyone say this? If so, what do you think might be reasons people say this? (Be *grace*ful when answering this.)

Now read Galatians 3:19-25, and discuss the following:

• In what ways has Jesus freed you from the need to be a "good person," and how has that made you a *better* person?

• Based on our passage today and your own experience of God's grace, what's one thing you can do to make God's grace more visible to the "good people" in your life?

# TOUCHING YOUR WORLD (25 minutes)

Review the following "weekly challenge" options, and select the challenge you'd like to do. Turn to a partner, and share your choice. Then make plans to connect with your partner sometime between now and the next session to check in and encourage one another.

☐ **THANK GOD FOR HIS GRACE.** Read the lyrics to the song "Amazing Grace" (you can find the lyrics pretty easily by using an online search engine). Think through what each verse means to you. Close your eyes and say or sing the lyrics as a prayer of thanksgiving to God. Consider writing a few verses of your own to add to the song. Don't worry about rhyming—just take the opportunity to thank God for some of the ways he has specifically brought his grace into your life.

☐ **COME UP WITH YOUR OWN METAPHOR FOR GRACE.** In this lesson, we used the torn-up picture and the perfect picture to show the distinctions between the law and grace. Look around your home and come up with objects that can be used as a metaphor to describe grace. This week, use your metaphor to explain grace to someone you know. (Even if someone already knows the definition of grace, it's worthwhile to be reminded of it...again and again.)

☐ **PASS GOD'S GRACE ALONG.** Many people—even those who attend church—still believe that the way into heaven is through good works. Ask your family members and close friends these simple questions: "If you died tonight, do you think you'd go to heaven? Why or why not?" If you get an answer like "I'll get to heaven because I'm a good person," read Romans 3:23 and Galatians 3:1-25 with that person. Talk through some of the things you learned in today's study, and talk especially about how God's grace has changed your own life.

Come together as a group. Share prayer requests, and then pray for everyone's needs. Pray that God would help each person in your group rely more and more on his gift of grace.

## Until next time...

Date _____

Time _____

Place _____

### Taking It Home:

**1.** Set a goal for how many times you'll either read through or watch on your DVD the Session 4 Bible passage (Galatians 3:26–4:11). Make a point to read the "A Sense of History" feature in Session 4 (page 42) before the next session. You may also want to review this week's passage as well—or even watch the entire book of Galatians straight through. (It takes about 24 minutes.) Let your weekly challenge partner know what goals you've set so he or she can encourage you and help hold you accountable.

**2.** Touch base sometime before the next session with your weekly challenge partner to compare notes on how you're both doing with the goals you've set.

**3.** If you have volunteered for a role or signed up to help with food or supplies for the next session, be sure to prepare for this. The Session 4 supplies list can be found on page 38, and the Food Coordinator instructions are on page 103.

**4. I commit to touching my world this week by discovering and sharing God's grace in the following ways:**

_____

_____

_____

# SESSION 4:

# GROWING INTO FREEDOM

GALATIANS 3:26–4:11

In this session, you'll learn about the importance of maturing in the freedom we have in Jesus.

---

## PRE-SESSION CHECKLIST:

☐ **Leader:** Check out the Session 4 Leader Notes in the back of the book (page 94).

☐ **Food Coordinator:** If you are responsible for the Session 4 snack, see page 103.

☐ **Supplies:**

- None

---

# *TASTE AND SEE* (20 minutes)

Grab some cake and a cup of coffee, and take a seat. Don't start eating your snack until your Leader instructs you to. Once your Leader gives the go-ahead, be sure to follow his or her instructions very closely. Afterward, discuss the following questions.

- What were you thinking while you ate your dessert according to such precise directions?


- What person would you say gave you the most instruction as a child? How good were you at following those instructions? Give examples.


- How did those childhood instructions help prepare you for adult life? In what ways do you wish they'd been more helpful?

 Watch the fourth chapter on the DVD (Galatians 3:26–4:11).

# Galatians 3:26–4:11 (NLT)

26For you are all children of God through faith in Christ Jesus. 27And all who have been united with Christ in baptism have put on the character of Christ, like putting on new clothes. 28There is no longer Jew or Gentile, slave or free, male and female. For you are all one in Christ Jesus. 29And now that you belong to Christ, you are the true children of Abraham. You are his heirs, and God's promise to Abraham belongs to you.

1Think of it this way. If a father dies and leaves an inheritance for his young children, those children are not much better off than slaves until they grow up, even though they actually own everything their father had. 2They have to obey their guardians until they reach whatever age their father set. 3And that's the way it was with us before Christ came. We were like children; we were slaves to the basic spiritual principles of this world. 4But when the right time came, God sent his Son, born of a woman, subject to the law. 5God sent him to buy freedom for us who were slaves to the law, so that he could adopt us as his very own children. 6And because we are his children, God has sent the Spirit of his Son into our hearts, prompting us to call out, "Abba, Father." 7Now you are no longer a slave but God's own child. And since you are his child, God has made you his heir.

[8]Before you Gentiles knew God, you were slaves to so-called gods that do not even exist. [9]So now that you know God (or should I say, now that God knows you), why do you want to go back again and become slaves once more to the weak and useless spiritual principles of the world? [10]You are trying to earn favor with God by observing certain days or months or seasons or years. [11]I fear for you. Perhaps all my hard work with you was for nothing.

# A SENSE OF HISTORY

### It's *Your* Inheritance

In this passage, Paul tells the Galatians that before they were Christians, they were no better than sons who had yet to inherit their father's estate. In doing so, he was referring to a Roman legal process of inheritance.

The process applied to heirs under the age of 14, who were to be placed under the control of a tutor until they turned 14. The tutor was chosen by the father and named in the will. After the child turned 14, he was placed under the control of a curator until he turned 25 (or another age designated by the father in the will).

Once the heir turned 25, *then* he was able to fully inherit his father's possessions. But until that time, he was under the control of the tutor or the curator—and so was his money. Imagine having a great treasure and being unable to use any of it, as well as having your entire life—and the use of *your* money—decided by someone else.

Paul tells his readers that before they were Christians, they were like that underage heir—unable to fully possess what was rightfully theirs and under the control of others (for Jews, the Law; for Gentiles, pagan rituals and ceremonies). Now that they are Christians, though, they are free. So why in the world, Paul asks, would they want to go back to being like those underage children? Why would Jews wish to go back into slavery under the Law? And why would Gentiles want to trade in their slavery to the pagan gods for the slavery of the Mosaic Law?

Take hold of your inheritance! That's what Paul begs his readers to do.

# DIGGING INTO SCRIPTURE (30 minutes)

As a group, discuss:

- What thoughts or emotions came to your mind as you watched this session's Bible passage just now or during the past week?

Now break into subgroups.

**Subgroup Leaders:** Use a maximum of 20 minutes for your discussion time.

Everyone in the subgroup should stand up. Everyone *but* the Subgroup Leader should put down his or her book and then obey the following orders as your Subgroup Leader reads them aloud:

- **Jump up and down on one foot.**

- **OK, spin around in a circle while you're still jumping up and down on one foot.**

- **Now pat your head with one hand and rub your tummy with the other as you continue spinning and jumping up and down on one foot.**

- **Now stick your tongue out, pat your head and rub your tummy, spin in a circle, and jump up and down on one foot.**

- **Now sing the alphabet song as you stick your tongue out, pat your head and rub your tummy, spin in a circle, and jump up and down on one foot.**

- **STOP!**

Once your head stops spinning and you can catch your breath, discuss the following questions:

- Honestly, how did you feel as you followed these commands?
- Describe a time you felt like you were jumping through hoops—doing silly, crazy things—to keep a relationship (or project or career) intact. What was that like? What was the end result?

Read Galatians 4:1-11 and then discuss the following:

- In what ways have you been "slaves to so-called gods that do not even exist"? In what ways do you *still* feel like a slave? How do you think this affects the way you approach God?

- We often think of a mature person as someone who's able to follow the rules or "the way things are done." In what ways is this true? In what ways isn't it?

- What's the connection between being a *child* of God and being a *mature* Christian?

- What does it mean to *you* to be God's child? What's one way—either verbally or through your actions—that you can express to others what that means?

Come together as a large group and share any highlights or questions from your subgroup discussion.

# *MAKING IT PERSONAL* (15 minutes)

Read Romans 8:15-17a in the margin, and then discuss the following
questions:

- In what ways do you feel like a slave in your day-to-day life?
  in your relationship with God?

> "*So you have not
> received a spirit that
> makes you fearful
> slaves. Instead, you
> received God's Spirit
> when he adopted you as
> his own children. Now we
> call him, 'Abba, Father.'
> For his Spirit joins with
> our spirit to affirm that
> we are God's children.
> And since we are his
> children, we are his
> heirs. In fact, together
> with Christ we are heirs
> of God's glory.*"
> —Romans 8:15-17a

- If you woke up tomorrow morning and you were suddenly
  no longer a "slave" in that area or areas, what would that
  look like?

- What keeps you from truly identifying yourself as a child of God? What's one
  thing you could do to begin to make that more of a reality in your life?

# *TOUCHING YOUR WORLD* (25 minutes)

Review the following "weekly challenge" options, and select the challenge you'd like to do. Turn to a partner, and share your choice. Then make plans to connect with your partner sometime between now and the next session to check in and encourage one another.

☐ **EXAMINE THE RITUALS IN YOUR LIFE.** Some faith-related rituals are wonderful—they give us regular and familiar ways of spending time with God. But when a ritual becomes simply routine or something that causes guilt, then there's a problem. Examine the rituals of your faith, whether it's thanking God for food, daily Scripture reading, or prayer walks. What do you connect with those times? If the words are positive, then keep those rituals. But if the words are negative (i.e. guilt, reluctance, obligation, indifference), then prayerfully consider eliminating those rituals for a time or altogether—or pray that God would breathe new life into them so they would again help you grow in your friendship with him.

☐ **RESEARCH THE FAITH RITUALS OF OTHERS.** Every religion has them. Spend some time with a friend or your weekly challenge partner this week researching faith rituals of Christians, as well as those of other religions. Talk together about what you find. You could even dialogue with someone of a different faith. Read Galatians 3:26–4:11, and discuss how the rituals you found might take them farther from God instead of bringing them closer. Think about how to instead bring God's grace into those situations.

☐ **LET GO OF YOUR EXPECTATIONS.** Are there any places where you're making others "jump through hoops"? Do you hold any of your family members, friends, or co-workers to an impossible standard? Do you judge them when they fall short? This week, watch yourself carefully as you interact with these people. Avoid making judgments. Extend the same grace to them that God has extended to you.

Come together as a group. Share prayer requests, and then pray for everyone's needs. Pray that God would help your group members fully embrace God's grace—and let go of the dead things that keep them from God.

## Until next time...

Date _____

Time _____

Place _____

### Taking It Home:

1. Make a point of watching the DVD Session 5 Bible passage (Galatians 4:12-31) and reading the "A Sense of History" feature in Session 5 (page 52) before the next session.

2. Touch base sometime before the next session with your weekly challenge partner to compare notes on how you're both doing with the goals you've set.

3. If you have volunteered for a role or signed up to help with food or supplies for the next session, be sure to prepare for this. The Session 5 supplies list can be found on page 48, and the Food Coordinator instructions are on page 103.

4. **I commit to touching my world this week by maturing in my freedom in Jesus in the following ways:**

_____

_____

_____

_____

# SESSION 5:
## SHARING IN GOD'S PROMISES

GALATIANS 4:12-31

In this session, you'll explore what it means to have *God's* promises, and how trusting in those promises can transform your relationships.

---

### PRE-SESSION CHECKLIST:

☐ **Leader:** Check out the Session 5 Leader Notes in the back of the book (page 95).

☐ **Food Coordinator:** If you are responsible for the Session 5 snack, see page 103.

☐ **Supplies:**
  • None

---

# *TASTE AND SEE* (20 minutes)

Before selecting your snack, break into subgroups.

Determine which subgroup has the youngest member. All subgroups but that one can go ahead and get some cookies. The subgroup with the youngest member gets today's healthy alternative—carrots.

Take a few minutes to share your snack in your subgroups and then come back together to discuss the following questions:

- **Carrot people:** What were you thinking as you watched the other subgroup(s) eating cookies?

> **Look on the bright side!**
>
> *Carrots have the highest natural sugar content of all vegetables except for beets.*

- **Cookie people:** What went through your mind as you ate your cookies and saw the other subgroup eating carrots?

- **Everyone:** What would your reaction be if your Leader now announced that all snacks would have to be dipped in dressing? Why?

 Watch the fifth chapter of the DVD (Galatians 4:12-31).

## Galatians 4:12-31 (NLT)

[12]Dear brothers and sisters, I plead with you to live as I do in freedom from these things, for I have become like you Gentiles— free from those laws.

You did not mistreat me when I first preached to you. [13]Surely you remember that I was sick when I first brought you the Good News. [14]But even though my condition tempted you to reject me, you did not despise me or turn me away. No, you took me in and cared for me as though I were an angel from God or even Christ Jesus himself. [15]Where is that joyful and grateful spirit you felt then? I am sure you would have taken out your own eyes and given them to me if it had been possible. [16]Have I now become your enemy because I am telling you the truth?

[17]Those false teachers are so eager to win your favor, but their intentions are not good. They are trying to shut you off from me so that you will pay attention only to them. [18]If someone is eager to do good things for you, that's all right; but let them do it all the time, not just when I'm with you.

[19]Oh, my dear children! I feel as if I'm going through labor pains for you again, and they will continue until Christ is fully developed in your lives. [20]I wish I were with you right now so I could change my tone. But at this distance I don't know how else to help you.

[21]Tell me, you who want to live under the law, do you know what the law actually says? [22]The Scriptures say that Abraham had two sons, one from his slave-wife and one from his freeborn wife. [23]The son of the slave-wife was born in a human attempt to bring about the fulfillment of God's promise. But the son of the freeborn wife was born as God's own fulfillment of his promise.

<sup>24</sup>These two women serve as an illustration of God's two covenants. The first woman, Hagar, represents Mount Sinai where people received the law that enslaved them. <sup>25</sup>And now Jerusalem is just like Mount Sinai in Arabia, because she and her children live in slavery to the law. <sup>26</sup>But the other woman, Sarah, represents the heavenly Jerusalem. She is the free woman, and she is our mother. <sup>27</sup>As Isaiah said,

"Rejoice, O childless woman,
>you who have never given birth!

Break into a joyful shout,
>you who have never been in labor!

For the desolate woman now has more children
>than the woman who lives with her husband!"

<sup>28</sup>And you, dear brothers and sisters, are children of the promise, just like Isaac. <sup>29</sup>But you are now being persecuted by those who want you to keep the law, just as Ishmael, the child born by human effort, persecuted Isaac, the child born by the power of the Spirit.

<sup>30</sup>But what do the Scriptures say about that? "Get rid of the slave and her son, for the son of the slave woman will not share the inheritance with the free woman's son." <sup>31</sup>So, dear brothers and sisters, we are not children of the slave woman; we are children of the free woman.

# A SENSE OF HISTORY

## *Hope for the Humiliated*

Like many couples, Sarah and Abraham wanted a son. But for them, a son would be more than a chance to try their hand at parenting; he would be their means of survival. In ancient Near Eastern culture, *kinship* drove the system. Jobs, income, social status, reputation, and relationships all depended on the prosperity of the family. And the prosperity of the family depended on two things: a rich and reputable heritage and making babies.

Sarah knew the consequences of these cultural "laws" quite well because she couldn't get pregnant (Genesis 11:30). So, as the years passed and Sarah's barrenness became more and more evident, she must have lived with an acute sense of inadequacy. Sarah couldn't provide for Abraham. She couldn't bolster the family pedigree with strapping boys. Sarah was *barren*; and everyone knew it. Even her servant Hagar knew it.

Because so much rested on Sarah's ability to have a child, her barrenness drove her and Abraham to make some hasty decisions. The Bible tells us of a number of these moments, including: Sarah offering Hagar to Abraham as a surrogate mother (Genesis 16:1-3); Sarah blaming Abraham when Hagar actually becomes pregnant (Genesis 16:5); Sarah harassing Hagar until Hagar is forced to run away, still carrying a child (Genesis 16:6); and finally, Sarah furiously demanding that Abraham cast out Hagar and Ishmael for good (Genesis 21:9-10). The cultural pressure on Sarah to produce an heir weighed so heavily on her that her life was clouded with impatience and discontentment.

In the end, however, through the promised child, Isaac, God gave Sarah *laughter* (Genesis 21:6-7). Paul points us to Sarah's story as an example of how we, too, are "children of the promise."

# DIGGING INTO SCRIPTURE (30 minutes)

As a group, discuss:

• What thoughts or emotions came to your mind as you watched this session's Bible passage just now or during the past week?

Now break into subgroups.

**Subgroup Leaders:** Find a place where your subgroup can talk with few distractions. Plan to come back together in 20 minutes.

Determine the person in your subgroup whose birthday is closest to today. That person will stay seated and extend his or her arms directly out to the side. Everyone else should stand on either side of this person, with an even number of people on each side. (If you don't have an even number of people standing, put the strongest person on your "short-handed" side.)

When everyone's in position, the seated person should try to raise his or her arms, while those standing push down on the seated person's arms (just enough so they can't be raised).

When you think the seated person has struggled enough, together let go of his or her arms. (Keep your heads out of the way of flying arms once you let go!) Take turns doing this activity, so everyone has a chance. Then sit together and discuss the following questions:

• Which activity was more enjoyable to you—trying to raise your arms or trying to hold someone else's arms down? Why?

• In what ways was your struggle to raise your arms like the ways we try to do things our own way, without God's help? How was the moment your arms were let go of like God's grace? How was it different?

Read Galatians 4:12-31, and discuss the following questions:
• Imagine being in Abraham and Sarah's situation—having received a promise from God but not seeing it fulfilled. How do you think you would have responded if you had been in their place?

• Think about a time God accomplished something through you, without (or well beyond) your own effort. What was that like? What did you learn from that experience?

• How does knowing that God *wants* to be involved in your life help you trust in his promises and *let* God be involved? How does it help us respond to others who *don't* trust in those promises?

Come together as a large group, and share any highlights or questions from your subgroup discussion.

# *MAKING IT PERSONAL* (15 minutes)

Write your name on the inside front of your BibleSense book (if you haven't already), and then pass your book clockwise around the group.

As you receive each person's book, write two encouraging notes in the back of the book. One note should describe one thing that makes the person valuable to *you*, and the other should describe one thing that makes him or her valuable to *God*.

> "*Yet true godliness with contentment is itself great wealth.*"
> —1 Timothy 6:6

Keep passing your books along until everyone's had a chance to write in every book. Take a few moments to read what people wrote to you. Then discuss the following questions:

- What thoughts crossed your mind as you read the entries in your book? How did it feel to be encouraged in this way?

- How did reading these encouragements remind you of how God is fulfilling his promises in your life even now?

- What are some other ways we can build each other up as a group more regularly?

# *TOUCHING YOUR WORLD* (25 minutes)

Review the following "weekly challenge" options, and select the challenge you'd like to do. Turn to a partner, and share your choice. Then make plans to connect with your partner sometime between now and the next session to check in and encourage one another.

☐ **PUT THE SHAME ON PAPER.** If this lesson has brought to mind times you believed lies about your personal value—whether they be from the media, co-workers, friends, family, or yourself—commit to writing them down and praying over them this week. If you're comfortable doing so, share what you find with your weekly challenge partner.

☐ **WRITE A LETTER TO MEND A STRAINED RELATIONSHIP.** The beauty of passages like Galatians 4:12-31 is that we discover that Paul struggled with hampered relationships just as we do. If you've recently had a fight with your spouse, one of your kids, or a friend, write an "epistle" of your own this week. Recount a fond memory, as Paul did. Use your letter to remind the receiver how valuable he or she is to you.

☐ **INVITE A NON-CHRISTIAN FRIEND TO DINNER.** You may know an unbelieving co-worker or friend who has felt ostracized by society or even by a church. Take this opportunity to show this person that God cares about the "outcast"—ask him or her to join you and a couple friends for a night of dinner and fun.

Come together as a group. Share prayer requests, and then pray for everyone's needs. Thank God for his promise of freedom and fulfillment to each of you. Pray that you can experience the pure laughter of Sarah and that your joy would be a message to others about Christ's freedom.

## Until next time...

Date _____

Time _____

Place _____

### Taking It Home:

1. Set a goal for how many times you'll either read through or watch on your DVD the Session 6 Bible passage (Galatians 5:1-15). Make a point to read the "A Sense of History" feature in Session 6 (page 61) before the next session. Let your weekly challenge partner know what goals you've set so he or she can encourage you and help hold you accountable.

2. Touch base sometime before the next session with your weekly challenge partner to compare notes on how you're both doing with the goals you've set.

3. If you have volunteered for a role or signed up to help with food or supplies for the next session, be sure to prepare for this. The Session 6 supplies list can be found on page 58, and the Food Coordinator instructions are on page 103.

4. **I commit to touching my world this week by sharing in God's promises in the following ways:**

_____

_____

_____

_____

# SESSION 6:

## PROTECTING YOUR FREEDOM

GALATIANS 5:1-15

**In this session, you'll look at ways to keep your freedom in Jesus safe from "big deals" that...*aren't*.**

## PRE-SESSION CHECKLIST:

☐ **Leader:** Check out the Session 6 Leader Notes in the back of the book (page 96).

☐ **Food Coordinator:** If you are responsible for the Session 6 snack, see page 103.

☐ **Supplies:**
- 1 recipe card for each subgroup

# TASTE AND SEE (20 minutes)

Choose only one drink and one snack. This isn't a buffet—"one of each" isn't an option today!

After you've chosen, look around and notice what other people chose to eat. Then discuss the following questions:

- Which items did you choose? Why those and not the others?

- What are some ways that eating food brings people closer together?

- What ways can you think of where food could actually be a barrier to certain relationships?

 Watch the sixth chapter on the DVD (Galatians 5:1-15).

## Galatians 5:1-15 (NLT)

[1]So Christ has truly set us free. Now make sure that you stay free, and don't get tied up again in slavery to the law.

[2]Listen! I, Paul, tell you this: If you are counting on circumcision to make you right with God, then Christ will be of no benefit to you. [3]I'll say it again. If you are trying to find favor with God by being circumcised, you must obey every regulation in the whole law of Moses. [4]For if you are trying to make yourselves right with God by keeping the law, you have been cut off from Christ! You have fallen away from God's grace.

[5]But we who live by the Spirit eagerly wait to receive by faith the righteousness God has promised to us. [6]For when we place our faith in Christ Jesus, there is no benefit in being circumcised or being uncircumcised. What is important is faith expressing itself in love.

[7]You were running the race so well. Who has held you back from following the truth? [8]It certainly isn't God, for he is the one who called you to freedom. [9]This false teaching is like a little yeast that spreads through the whole batch of dough! [10]I am trusting the Lord to keep you from believing false teachings. God will judge that person, whoever he is, who has been confusing you. [11]Dear brothers and sisters, if I were still preaching that you must be circumcised—as some say I do—why am I still being persecuted? If I were no longer preaching salvation through the cross of Christ, no one would be offended. [12]I just wish that those troublemakers who want to mutilate you by circumcision would mutilate themselves.

¹³For you have been called to live in freedom, my brothers and sisters. But don't use your freedom to satisfy your sinful nature. Instead, use your freedom to serve one another in love. ¹⁴For the whole law can be summed up in this one command: "Love your neighbor as yourself." ¹⁵But if you are always biting and devouring one another, watch out! Beware of destroying one another.

## A SENSE OF HISTORY

### What's the Big Deal?

Paul is frustrated here—can you tell? He wanted the Galatians to be free in Jesus—not get wrapped up in following new laws. But that's exactly what these new Christians were doing. And the specific new law in this situation was the old law of circumcision.

To the Hebrew people, circumcision was a symbol of covenant with God and an act of religious purification. The tradition began when God commanded Abraham to be circumcised at age 99; afterward, all Hebrew boys were circumcised when they were eight days old. Even foreigners who wanted to join the Israelite community and all their male household members were required to submit to circumcision, no matter their age. Thus, the word *uncircumcised* carried an extremely negative connotation in Hebrew society.

In describing this situation, Bible scholar Scot McKnight wrote, "Legalism, according to Galatians...combined Christianity with [Judaism] in a way that demanded total commitment to Israel's law as the climax of one's conversion to Christ." No wonder Paul told the Galatians in verses 2 and 4, "If you are counting on circumcision to make you right with God, then...you have been cut off from Christ!"

# DIGGING INTO SCRIPTURE (30 minutes)

As a group, discuss:

• What thoughts or emotions came to your mind as you watched this session's Bible passage just now or during the past week?

Now break into subgroups.

**Leader:** Give each Subgroup Leader a recipe card.

**Subgroup Leaders:** Find a place where your subgroup can talk with few distractions. Plan to come back together in 20 minutes.

Your Subgroup Leader should read aloud *only* the title of your recipe card. Before reading the recipe itself, discuss as a subgroup how each of you would prepare the item on your card. (Hint: If your recipe for making pizza is, "Preheat oven and insert frozen pizza," that's OK!)

Once everyone has explained how he or she would prepare the item on your card, read the actual recipe. Then discuss the following:

• Did you agree on how to make this item? What instructions do you think would make a big difference in your final result? What instruction wouldn't?

> "*Sometimes we will have to say; 'Others may, I will not.' This is very different to saying 'I will not, so no one else will either!', which is using our own weaknesses to judge and condemn others.*"
>
> —George Verwer, founder of Operation Mobilization

• What are some "big-deal" items society disagrees about? What's truly important about these issues? What's not?

• How can these issues distract us from what's really important in our walk with Jesus?

Read Galatians 5:1-15, and discuss the following questions:
• What's something that was a "big deal" to you in the past—but now you wonder why? What did you learn from that experience?

• How is the freedom Paul talks about here (and elsewhere in Galatians) like or unlike the "freedom" most people think of when they hear the word? how are those differences like or unlike the argument he's making here?

# *MAKING IT PERSONAL* (15 minutes)

Designate a writer for your subgroup. Spend a couple minutes brainstorming about ways Christians get caught up in big deal issues that really aren't big deals, and have your writer keep a list. (Remember: when you're brainstorming, all ideas are accepted. This isn't the time to evaluate ideas or propose answers to the problems brought up.)

When your brainstorm session is over, discuss the following:

• Did any specific items catch your attention? Why?

Read Galatians 5:7-10 again, and discuss the following:

• When is it right to protect ourselves from the "yeast" of the world? When is it OK to stand up—as Paul does in this passage—and openly oppose a wrong influence instead of just walking away?

"[Jesus] also asked, 'What else is the Kingdom of God like? It is like the yeast a woman used in making bread. Even though she put only a little yeast in three measures of flour, it permeated every part of the dough.'"
—Luke 13:20-21

• What's one way you can influence the world around you positively, through the freedom we have in Jesus?

Come together as a large group, and share your most interesting thoughts and brainstorm ideas from your subgroup discussion.

# *TOUCHING YOUR WORLD* (25 minutes)

Review the following "weekly challenge" options, and select the challenge you'd like to do. Turn to a partner, and share your choice. Then make plans to connect with your partner sometime between now and the next session to check in and encourage one another.

☐ **REACH OUT TO SOMEONE FROM A DIFFERENT CHRISTIAN TRADITION.** Do you know someone from work, an organization you're involved in, or a neighbor who worships in a Christian tradition that's entirely different from yours? Take time to speak to this person—you might go out for coffee or lunch—and ask questions. Don't debate differences; take time to learn this person's story and traditions.

☐ **DENY YOUR SACRED COW.** Most people have a "sacred cow" they can't part with. Yours probably isn't circumcision, but what is it? First, determine what your sacred cow is, and then choose a specific way you can deny it this week. For instance, if *your* sacred cow is not smoking, join co-workers on their smoking break. (You don't have to *participate* in smoking, of course; just love the people who *do* smoke.) Or, if your sacred cow is a specific politically slanted radio show, don't listen to it this week (or spend time with someone from "the other side"). These practices will help to humanize the people who don't share your sacred cow and help you think more clearly about loving your neighbor.

☐ **AND WHO *IS* YOUR NEIGHBOR?** As you may remember from Christ's parable of the good Samaritan (Luke 10:25-37), neighbors are not always people you know! This week, put Galatians 5:14 into action, and help someone you don't know. It may be an elderly person at the grocery store who needs assistance with her groceries, a poor person downtown, or children in your neighborhood. Prayerfully keep your eyes open for opportunities in which you can love your neighbors!

Come back together as a group. Share prayer requests, and then pray for everyone's needs. Pray that God will help you to focus your freedom on building his kingdom, not simply following laws. Commit yourselves to loving your neighbors.

## Until next time...

Date _____

Time _____

Place _____

## Taking It Home:

1. Set a goal for how many times you'll either read through or watch on your DVD the Session 7 Bible passage (Galatians 5:16–6:6). Make a point to read the "A Sense of History" feature in Session 7 (page 72) before the next session. You may also want to review this week's passage as well—or even watch the entire book of Galatians straight through. (It takes about 24 minutes.) Let your weekly challenge partner know what goals you've set so he or she can encourage you and help hold you accountable.

2. Touch base sometime before the next session with your weekly challenge partner to compare notes on how you're both doing with the goals you've set.

**3.** If you have volunteered for a role or signed up to help with food or supplies for the next session, be sure to prepare for this. The Session 7 supplies list can be found on page 68, and the Food Coordinator instructions are on page 104.

**4. I commit to touching my world this week by using my freedom for God and others in the following ways:**

_____

_____

_____

_____

_____

# SESSION 7:

# BEARING GOOD FRUIT

GALATIANS 5:16–6:6

**In this session, you'll discuss how living in the Spirit helps to produce good fruit in our lives.**

## PRE-SESSION CHECKLIST:

☐ **Leader:** Check out the Session 7 Leader Notes in the back of the book (page 97).

☐ **Food Coordinator:** If you are responsible for the Session 7 snack, see page 104.

☐ **Supplies:**

- 1 recent newspaper for each subgroup

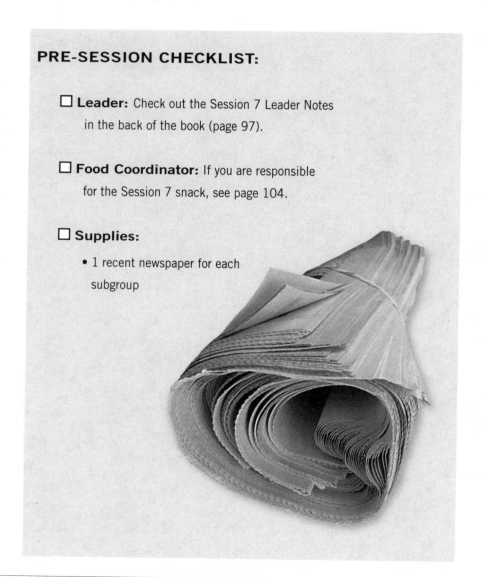

# *TASTE AND SEE* (20 minutes)

Before enjoying this session's snack, you're going to make a few judgments *about* your snack.

Gather the group around a table with all the fruit piled in the middle. Make your best guess, and vote on which fruit you think will be good and which will be sub par. (No touching!) As you vote, your Host will move the "good" fruit to one end of the table and the "inferior" fruit to the other.

After all the pieces are voted upon, take turns cutting them up. Each person should take two bowls and put samples from each side of the table into each bowl. As you eat, discuss the following questions:

- How accurately were you able to judge between the good fruit and the not-so-good fruit?

- What did you base your judgments on? (Be specific, where possible.)

- In your own life, what might someone see in you that would cause them to expect your life to bear "good fruit"?

 Watch the seventh chapter on the DVD (Galatians 5:16–6:6).

# Galatians 5:16–6:6 (NLT)

[16]So I say, let the Holy Spirit guide your lives. Then you won't be doing what your sinful nature craves. [17]The sinful nature wants to do evil, which is just the opposite of what the Spirit wants. And the Spirit gives us desires that are the opposite of what the sinful nature desires. These two forces are constantly fighting each other, so you are not free to carry out your good intentions. [18]But when you are directed by the Spirit, you are not under obligation to the law of Moses.

[19]When you follow the desires of your sinful nature, the results are very clear: sexual immorality, impurity, lustful pleasures, [20]idolatry, sorcery, hostility, quarreling, jealousy, outbursts of anger, selfish ambition, dissension, division, [21]envy, drunkenness, wild parties, and other sins like these. Let me tell you again, as I have before, that anyone living that sort of life will not inherit the Kingdom of God.

[22]But the Holy Spirit produces this kind of fruit in our lives: love, joy, peace, patience, kindness, goodness, faithfulness, [23]gentleness, and self-control. There is no law against these things!

[24]Those who belong to Christ Jesus have nailed the passions and desires of their sinful nature to his cross and crucified them there. [25]Since we are living by the Spirit, let us follow the Spirit's leading in every part of our lives. [26]Let us not become conceited, or provoke one another, or be jealous of one another.

¹Dear brothers and sisters, if another believer is overcome by some sin, you who are godly should gently and humbly help that person back onto the right path. And be careful not to fall into the same temptation yourself. ²Share each other's burdens, and in this way obey the law of Christ. ³If you think you are too important to help someone, you are only fooling yourself. You are not that important.

⁴Pay careful attention to your own work, for then you will get the satisfaction of a job well done, and you won't need to compare yourself to anyone else. ⁵For we are each responsible for our own conduct.

⁶Those who are taught the word of God should provide for their teachers, sharing all good things with them.

# A SENSE OF HISTORY
## Tracking the Holy Spirit

Jesus said of the Holy Spirit, "The wind blows wherever it wants. Just as you can hear the wind but can't tell where it comes from or where it is going, so you can't explain how people are born of the Spirit" (John 3:8). So how does one track this untrackable Spirit? By paying careful attention to the evidence the Spirit leaves behind!

In the second verse of the Bible, "the Spirit of God" was hovering over the earth's surface. The evidence the Spirit left behind was Creation! Later in the Old Testament, we find the Holy Spirit connected with prophecy. Isaiah said, "The Spirit of the Sovereign Lord is upon me" (Isaiah 61:1); Micah said, "I am filled with power—with the Spirit of the Lord" (Micah 3:8); and when Ezekiel went to the valley of dry bones, he said, "I was carried away by the Spirit of the Lord" (Ezekiel 37:1). In these passages, the evidence the Spirit left behind was the powerful words that both comforted and challenged the people and predicted the coming of the Messiah.

Shortly after Christ's death the Holy Spirit became evident in an even more powerful way. On the day of Pentecost, the Spirit came as a "mighty windstorm" (Acts 2:2) and gave people many gifts to minister in Christ's name (1 Corinthians 12). The Spirit helped the disciples know what to say (Acts 4:8), strengthened martyrs (Acts 7:55), directed their mission (Acts 8:29, 39; 13:2; 16:6-7), and as we see in this passage, empowered them to live righteous lives. The evidence was a church that thrived even in the midst of persecution.

# DIGGING INTO SCRIPTURE (30 minutes)

As a group, discuss:

• What thoughts or emotions came to your mind as you watched this session's Bible passage just now or during the past week?

> **"**Man is the only animal that blushes—or needs to.**"**
>
> —Mark Twain

Now break into subgroups.

**Leader:** Give a newspaper to each subgroup. Try to have at least four people in each subgroup.

**Subgroup leaders:** Find a place where your subgroup can talk with few distractions. Plan to come back together in 20 minutes.

Now, break up your subgroup even further. One half of your subgroup should look for stories in the newspaper that illustrate how bad people can be; the other half should look for stories that illustrate how good people can be. Take five minutes to look through your section(s) of newspaper, and then talk for a few minutes about the articles you found.

Afterward, come back together in your subgroup to discuss the following:

- How did each set of stories make you feel about the human race? Why? What articles did you find where *both* the goodness and evil of people were in evidence?

> "*It is interesting that the Bible talks of the* fruit *of the Spirit rather than* fruits. *A tree may bear many apples, but all come from the same tree. In the same way, the Holy Spirit is the source of all fruit in our lives.*"
>
> —Billy Graham

Read Galatians 5:16-26 and then discuss the following questions:

- What does Paul say makes the crucial difference between whether our lives produce good or bad fruit? What does that look like to you personally?

- In this ongoing fight between the desires of the sinful nature and the Holy Spirit, what "round" do you think that fight is in your own life?

- In what ways does it seem like your "old sinful nature" hits below the belt? What can you do to better prepare yourself for those times?

- What can you do to "go on the offensive" in this battle? How can other Christians help you fight this battle?

Come together as a large group, and share any highlights or questions from your subgroup discussion.

# *MAKING IT PERSONAL* (15 minutes)

Read Galatians 6:1-6, and discuss the following questions:

- How does bearing each other's burdens "obey the law of Christ"? What's the difference between *this* law and other laws we've discussed in this study?

- Look one more time at the list in Galatians 5:22-23. Which of these fruits are most evident in your own life? Which fruits do you think could use a little more fertilizer?

- What are some practical ways we can "share each other's troubles and problems," either as a group or as individuals, in the world around us?

# *TOUCHING YOUR WORLD* (25 minutes)

Review the following "weekly challenge" options, and select the challenge you'd like to do. Turn to a partner, and share your choice. Then make plans to connect with your partner sometime between now and the next session to check in and encourage one another.

☐ **WORK ON YOUR "FRUIT CROP."** Share which of the fruit of the Spirit you need to work on most in your life. Then focus your prayer and devotional life on that area of your life in the coming week. For instance, if it's patience you need to work on, pray for patience, especially seeking the help of the Holy Spirit in this area. To take this to the next level, focus each day on a different life situation in which you have the opportunity to show more patience.

☐ **AFFIRM THE GOOD FRUIT YOU SEE OTHERS PRODUCE.** Affirmation is a powerful tool. Some people go around trying to catch other people doing wrong, but Jesus often sought to "catch people doing right" (see Matthew 8:5-10; 16:13-17; Luke 22:28-30; John 1:47). Focus on one or two of the fruit of the Spirit listed in Galatians 5:22-23. Make a special effort this week to affirm people every time you see them displaying these fruit in their lives.

☐ **GET HELP WITH A MORAL STRUGGLE *YOU* ARE HAVING.** Examine the list of "evil" results in Galatians 5:19-21. Are you really having trouble in one of those areas right now? Confess it to a trusted Christian friend, and together plan a strategy for winning this battle.

☐ **CALL OR VISIT A STRUGGLING PERSON.** Who do you know who's going through a tough time right now? Set aside some time to get together with that person, and focus on just listening. What is causing him or her pain right now? What moral issues is this person struggling with? What can you do to share his or her troubles and problems and encourage them?

Come back together as a group. Share prayer requests, and then pray for everyone's needs. Pray especially that your group can effectively support each other in the midst of your struggles.

## Until next time...

Date _____

Time _____

Place _____

## Taking It Home:

**1.** Set a goal for how many times you'll either read through or watch on your DVD the Session 8 Bible passage (Galatians 6:7-18). Make a point to read the "A Sense of History" feature in Session 8 (page 82) before the next session. You may also want to review this week's passage as well—or even watch the entire book of Galatians straight through. (It takes about 24 minutes.) Let your weekly challenge partner know what goals you've set so he or she can encourage you and help hold you accountable.

**2.** Touch base sometime before the next session with your weekly challenge partner to compare notes on how you're both doing with the goals you've set.

**3.** If you volunteered for a role or signed up to help with food or supplies for the next session, be sure to prepare for this. The Session 8 supplies list can be found on page 78, and the Food Coordinator instructions are on page 104.

**4. I commit to touching my world this week by bearing good fruit in the following ways:**

_____

_____

_____

_____

# SESSION 8:

# PREPARING FOR THE HARVEST

GALATIANS 6:7-18

**In this final session, you'll learn about the "equipment" you need to have a productive "harvest" in Jesus.**

## PRE-SESSION CHECKLIST:

☐ **Leader:** Check out the Session 8 Leader Notes in the back of the book (page 98).

☐ **Food Coordinator:** If you are responsible for the Session 8 snack, see page 104.

☐ **Supplies:**

- different packet of seeds for each group member

- medium-size planter filled with soil for each subgroup

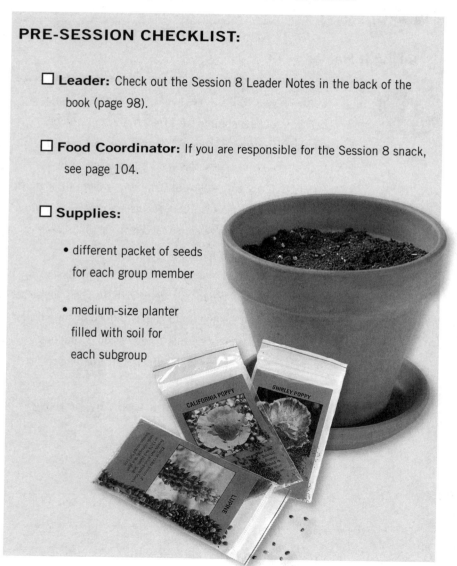

# *TASTE AND SEE* (20 minutes)

Choose from the selection of dried fruit and nuts provided. As you eat, read the note in the margin, and then discuss the following questions:

- Which of the benefits of your snack listed here are most important for you personally? What other benefits can you think of?

- Why might a diet such as this have been important to the *original* readers of Galatians?

- One of the benefits of dried fruit and nuts mentioned here is that they will last a long time. What are you doing right now that you're confident will outlast you?

> ***Did you know?*** *Dried fruit and nuts are a primary export of Turkey, the modern country where Galatia was located, to the United States. The benefits of these foods include:*
> - *healthy alternative to sweets, confectioneries, and candies*
> - *long shelf life*
> - *lightweight and easily transportable*
> - *ideal for rural distribution (no refrigeration or special handling needed)*

 Watch the final chapter on the DVD (Galatians 6:7-18).

# Galatians 6:7-18 (NLT)

⁷Don't be misled—you cannot mock the justice of God. You will always harvest what you plant. ⁸Those who live only to satisfy their own sinful nature will harvest decay and death from that sinful nature. But those who live to please the Spirit will harvest everlasting life from the Spirit. ⁹So let's not get tired of doing what is good. At just the right time we will reap a harvest of blessing if we don't give up. ¹⁰Therefore, whenever we have the opportunity, we should do good to everyone—especially to those in the family of faith.

¹¹Notice what large letters I use as I write these closing words in my own handwriting.

¹²Those who are trying to force you to be circumcised want to look good to others. They don't want to be persecuted for teaching that the cross of Christ alone can save. ¹³And even those who advocate circumcision don't really keep the whole law themselves. They only want you to be circumcised so they can boast about it and claim you as their disciples.

¹⁴As for me, may I never boast about anything except the cross of our Lord Jesus Christ. Because of that cross, my interest in this world has been crucified, and the world's interest in me has also died. ¹⁵It doesn't matter whether we have been circumcised or not. What counts is whether we have been transformed into a new creation. ¹⁶May God's peace and mercy be upon all who live by this principle; they are the new people of God.

<sup>17</sup>From now on, don't let anyone trouble me with these things. For I bear on my body the scars that show I belong to Jesus.

<sup>18</sup>Dear brothers and sisters, may the grace of our Lord Jesus Christ be with your spirit. Amen.

# A SENSE OF HISTORY

## *Farming in Biblical Times*

As previously mentioned, Galatia was located in what is now Turkey, where Paul helped found churches in Iconium, Lystra, and Derbe (see Acts 14). Sowing and reaping were essential activities in that land, as they were in most places during New Testament times. Since there were no stores conveniently stocking frozen, canned, and preserved produce, most people depended upon the harvest from the soil their own hands had worked. Even many people who lived in the towns also worked in the field beyond the city wall.

Tools were primitive, and work was slow. Ploughs, which were generally pulled by oxen or mules, usually had a single point made of iron and could turn only one furrow at a time. The farmer needed strength to control the animals to keep the furrows straight. He swung a sickle to harvest crops, and his hands must have been heavily callused.

As farming was a common occupation in biblical times, it was also a rich source of imagery for teaching. Jesus spoke of a tree and its fruit (Matthew 7:15-20) and the need for laborers for a good spiritual harvest (Matthew 9:35-38), and he told the parables of the sower and the wheat and weeds (Matthew 13:1-30). Paul also used farming imagery. For example, he told the Corinthians that the one who sows sparingly will reap sparingly (2 Corinthians 9:6).

Today Turkey's varied climates and adequate rainfall permit a broad range of crops, including many cereal grains, as well as fruit and nuts, and it is likely that was the case in Paul's time as well.

# *DIGGING INTO SCRIPTURE* (30 minutes)

As a group, discuss:

• What thoughts or emotions came to your mind as you watched this session's Bible passage, whether just now or during the past week?

• What have your overall impressions been as you've interacted with the book of Galatians? How has God spoken to you through this study?

Now break into subgroups.

**Leader:** Give a packet of seeds to every person, and give a planter filled with planting soil to each subgroup.

**Subgroup leaders:** Find a place where your subgroup can talk with few distractions. Plan to come back together in 20 minutes.

Examine the seed packets you've been given. Pass them around your subgroup. Look at the pictures of the plants the seeds are supposed to produce, and read the planting instructions for each one. Then discuss the following:

> *"Oh, Adam was a gardener, and God who made him sees*
> *That half a proper gardener's work is done upon his knees,*
> *So when your work is finished, you can wash your hands and pray*
> *For the Glory of the Garden, that it may not pass away!"*
>
> —Rudyard Kipling,
> "The Glory of the Garden"

- Which of these plants do you like best? Why? What are some of the benefits of each plant?

Plant some of your seeds in your planter, taking care to plant at the suggested depth for each and to leave room for the other group members' seeds. Then discuss the following questions:

- How important do you think the planting instructions are? What do you think would happen if your seeds were planted at different depths or with less space around them?

- How patient are you with growing things? What can cause discouragement when one is gardening or farming?

> *"Christlikeness is not produced by imitation, but by inhabitation. We allow Christ to live through us."*
>
> —Rick Warren,
> The Purpose-Driven Life

Read Galatians 6:7-18, and answer the following questions:

• When have you seen a "harvest of blessing" as a result of living in the Spirit? How does it line up with what Paul says in this passage?

• When have you been discouraged while "doing what is good"? What (or who) has helped you during those times?

• What work is taking up a lot of your time and energy right now—your job, home, family, church? How can we re-energize when we're tired of working?

Come back together as a large group, and discuss any highlights and insights from your subgroup time.

# *MAKING IT PERSONAL* (15 minutes)

Discuss the following questions:

• Paul normally had a secretary write his letters. Why do you think it was important for him to personalize this message by writing in his own hand (see verse 11)?

• What's one opportunity you have right now to do good for someone else—to put your signature on his or her life? What spiritual or hands-on help do you need to make that a reality?

• As a result of what you've learned in these sessions, what life change would you sign your name to right now? Write it below, and sign your name to it.

Take your packet of seeds home with you as a reminder of what God has already started in you.

Also, if you are going to continue as a group after this week, put your planter in a window of the home where you meet, so group members can check its progress each week. If you are not going to continue as a group, take your planter to your church, and find a window where you can display it. Make sure someone is assigned to water and care for it. Let these plants be a symbol of your continued growth in Jesus!

# *TOUCHING YOUR WORLD* (25 minutes)

Review the following "weekly challenge" options, and select the challenge you'd like to do. Turn to a partner, and share your choice. Then make plans to connect with your partner sometime in the next week to check in and encourage one another.

☐ **MAKE A SPIRITUAL-GROWTH CHART.** Parents often put a growth chart for their children on a wall and periodically mark their height. Make something similar for your own spiritual-growth chart. Record the events or experiences in your life that really changed you, working your way from past to the present. Then look it over. Thank God for what he has done in your life, and prayerfully consider what the next step should be for you as you continue to become "a new creation."

☐ **TAKE TIME WITH A FRIEND FOR MUTUAL ENCOURAGEMENT.** Paul tells us, "So let's not get tired of doing what is good. At just the right time we will reap a harvest of blessing if we don't give up" (Galatians 6:9). The best way to fight discouragement is mutual encouragement. Find someone who's discouraged or overwhelmed right now, and share a positive word about how God can produce fruit in his or her life even through this present situation.

☐ **INVEST IN A "PEOPLE HARVEST."** You can define this "harvest" in a number of ways: people whom you influence to make a commitment to Jesus Christ, people who grow spiritually because of something you say or do, or people whose lives are enriched physically or emotionally because of something you have done. Set a goal for the number of people you touch in one of these ways (or in some other way God's leading you in).

Come back together as a group. Share prayer requests, and then pray for everyone's needs. Pray especially that your group can effectively support each other in the midst of your struggles.

**Leader:** If you haven't already, take some time to discuss what's next for the group. Will you stay together and work on another BibleSense book? Will you celebrate your time together with a party and be done? Or will you have a party, and *then* start another BibleSense book the following week? Set a date, time, and place to get together with your weekly challenge partner during the next week.

## Until next time:

Date _____

Time _____

Place _____

## Taking It Home:

1. Touch base during the week with your weekly challenge partner to compare notes on how you're both doing with the goals you've set.

2. You may want to review this week's passage—or even watch the entire book of Galatians straight through on your DVD, now that you've finished your study. (It takes about 24 minutes to watch the entire book.)

**3. I commit to touching my world this week by improving my spiritual harvest in the following ways:**

_____

_____

_____

_____

# NOTES & ROLES

# CONTENTS

## LEADER NOTES

## GROUP ROLES

# LEADER NOTES

## GENERAL LEADER TIPS

1. Although these sessions are designed to require minimum advance preparation, try to read over each session ahead of time and watch the DVD chapter for that session. Highlight any questions you feel are especially important for your group to spend time on during the session.

2. Prior to the first session, watch the "Leading a BibleSense Session" overview on the DVD. You'll notice that this isn't your average Bible study. Food? Activities? Don't forget that Jesus used food and everyday items and experiences in *his* small group all the time. Jesus' disciples certainly weren't comfortable when he washed their feet (John 13:5-17), and were even a bit confused at first. Jesus reassured them, "You don't understand now what I am doing, but someday you will" (verse 7), and it turned out to be a powerful lesson that stayed with them the rest of their lives. It's our prayer that your group will have similar experiences.

3. Take the time to read the group roles on pages 99-108, and make sure all critical tasks and roles are covered for each session. The three roles you *absolutely need filled* for each session are Leader, Host, and Food Coordinator. These roles can be rotated around the group, if you like.

4. Discuss as a group how to handle child care—not only because it can be a sensitive subject, but also to give your group an opportunity to begin working together *as* a group. See the Child Care Coordinator tips on page 108 for ideas on how to handle this important issue.

5. Don't be afraid to ask for volunteers. Who knows—they may want to commit to a role once they've tried it (and if it's available on a regular basis). However, give people the option of "no thanks" as well.

6. Every session will begin with a snack, so work closely with your Food Coordinator—he or she has a vital role in each session. If you need to, go ahead

and ask for donations from your group for the snacks that are provided each week.

7. Always start on time. If you do this from Session 1, you'll avoid the group arriving and starting later as the study goes on.

8. Be ready and willing to pray at times other than the closing time. Start each session with prayer—let everyone know they're getting "down to business." Be open to other times prayer is appropriate, such as when someone answers a question and ends up expressing pain or grief over a situation he or she's currently struggling with. Don't save prayer for the end—stop and pray right there and then. Your Prayer Coordinator can take the lead in these situations, if you like, but give him or her "permission" to do so.

9. Try not to have the first or last word on every question (or even most of them). Give everyone the opportunity to participate. At the same time, don't put anyone on the spot. Remind group members that they can pass on any questions they're not comfortable answering.

10. Keep things on track. There are suggested time limits for each section. Encourage good discussion, but don't be afraid to "rope 'em back in." If you do decide to spend extra time on a question or activity, consider skipping or spending less time on a later question or activity so you can stay on schedule.

11. Don't let your group off the hook with the assignments in the "Touching Your World" section—this is when group members get to apply in a personal way what they have learned. Encourage group members to follow through on their assignments. You may even want to make it a point to ask how they did with their weekly challenges during snack time at the beginning of your next session.

12. Also note that the last weekly challenge in "Touching Your World" is often an outreach assignment that can be done either individually or as a group. Make sure that group members who take on these challenges are encouraged—and if it's a group activity, organized. If your group has an Outreach Coordinator, let him or her take the lead here, and touch base regularly.

13. Lastly, the single most important thing a leader can do for his or her group is to spend time in prayer for group members. Why not take a minute and pray for your group right now?

## Session 1 Leader Notes

1. Read the General Leader Tips starting on page 89, if you haven't already. Take a peek at the tips for other group roles as well (pages 99-108).

2. Make sure everyone has a BibleSense book and DVD. Have the group pass around their books to record contact information (page 7) before or during "Taste and See" or at the end of the session.

3. If this is the first time you're meeting as a group, you may want to take a few minutes before your session to lay down some ground rules. Here are three simple ones:
   - Don't say anything that will embarrass anyone or violate someone's trust.
   - Likewise, anything shared in the group *stays* in the group, unless the person sharing it says otherwise.
   - No one has to answer a question he or she is uncomfortable answering.

4. Take time to review the group roles on pages 99-108 before you get together, and be ready to discuss them at the end of your session. Assign as many roles as you can, but don't pressure anyone to take on something he or she doesn't want or isn't yet sure about.

5. For this session, you're responsible for the items in the Supplies list on page 8. You'll want to assign the Supplies list for future sessions. The Host is the most sensible choice to handle this responsibility, or it can be rotated around the group.

6. For the activity in "Digging Into Scripture," use good sense in your magazine choices. Pick out magazines that advertise viewpoints that wouldn't line up with Scripture, but make sure there's nothing that would potentially offend group members.

7. Notice the index cards in the Supplies list for this session. Keep some handy in case anyone in your group wants to use them for the "Decide what side you're on" option in "Touching Your World."

8. Unless you're ahead of the game and already have a Food Coordinator, you're responsible for the snack for this first session. You'll want to make sure you have a Food Coordinator for future sessions, but for this session, be sure to review the Food Coordinator assignment on page 102.

9. Before you dismiss this first session, make a special point to remind group members of the importance of following through on the weekly challenge they committed to in the "Touching Your World" section.

## Session 2 Leader Notes

1. If new people join the group this session, use part of the "Taste and See" time to ask them to introduce themselves to the group, and have the group pass around their books to record contact information (page 7). Give a brief summary of the points covered in Session 1.

2. Take note of the sensory experience in "Digging into Scripture." **For Extra Impact:** Play a quick target game with the cereal by seeing how many times (in one minute) your subgroup can fling pieces of cereal with a spoon across the room into a bowl. Use this experience to talk about the reality of imperfection in a Christian's life—no matter how hard you try, you aren't likely to "hit the target" every time.

3. If you told the group during the first session that you'd be following up to see how they did with their Touching Your World commitment, be sure to do so. This is an opportunity to establish an environment of accountability. However, be prepared to share how you did with your *own* commitment from the first session.

4. For the closing prayer time, ask for volunteers to pray for requests that group members shared. You may want to ask the Prayer Coordinator in advance to lead the prayer time. If you don't have a Prayer Coordinator and will lead the prayer time, look over the Prayer Coordinator tips on page 106, and keep them in mind. If you ask someone else to lead, try to ask in advance. Direct that person to the Prayer Coordinator tips. Also, if your group has decided to use a prayer list, make sure you use it during the prayer time.

## Session 3 Leader Notes

1. Note the Supplies list and the sensory experience in "Digging Into Scripture." Get these pictures from magazines, your family pictures, or anywhere else. Just make sure each subgroup has two identical pictures. If necessary, photocopy pictures or print multiple copies from your PC so you'll have enough matching pairs. This activity will likely have even more meaning if the picture shows someone or something that everyone in the subgroup will recognize.

2. Are you praying for your group members regularly? It's the most important thing a leader can do for his or her group. Take some time now to pray for your group, if you haven't already.

## Session 4 Leader Notes

1. Congratulations! You're halfway through this study. This is a good time for a checkup. How's the group going? What's worked well so far? What might you consider changing as you approach the remaining sessions?

2. On that note, you may find it helpful to make some notes right after the session to help you evaluate how the group is doing. Ask yourself, "Did everyone participate?" and "Is there anyone I need to make a special effort to follow up with before the next session?"

3. Take special note of the snack in "Taste and See" because you have a special role during snack time. Before the session, think of some special (realistic, but annoying) instructions group members should follow to eat their snack. For example, "Take one bite from the right corner of your cheesecake….Now eat a piece of the fruit on top of the cheesecake….Now take a sip of coffee." Continue until everyone has finished eating a slice of cheesecake. You'll probably get some unpleasant comments and looks, but carry on anyway, making sure everyone obeys your every command!

4. Take similar note of the sensory experience in "Digging Into Scripture." Instruct your Subgroup Leaders beforehand to spend no more than 15 seconds on each listed action. And encourage your subgroups to stick with it here—let them know there's a method to the seeming madness of this activity.

## Session 5 Leader Notes

1. Remember the importance of starting and ending on time, and remind your group of it, too, if you need to.

2. Note the activity in "Making It Personal." If the group is too large, you can conduct this activity in subgroups instead. Make sure to have enough pens or pencils for everyone in the group. Encourage your group (or your Subgroup Leaders) to spend a few extra minutes on the last question in this section. Suggest that people really brainstorm about it and then think of a way to put at least one of the ideas into action.

3. Remind group members of the importance of following through on the weekly challenge each of them has committed to in "Touching Your World."

## Session 6 Leader Notes

1. See the Supplies list and the activity in "Digging Into Scripture." Have recipe cards to choose from, making sure the recipes are for items that people normally eat and are not too complicated. Suggest recipes for something that can be made a number of different ways—chili or an omelet, for example—which will make this activity more interesting.

2. How are you doing with your prayer time for the group? Take some time to pray for your group now, if you haven't done so already.

## Session 7 Leader Notes

1. Since your next session will be your group's last one in this book, you may want to start discussing with the group what to do after you complete this study.

2. On that note, you may want to do another group checkup before you begin your next study (if that's the plan). Ask yourself, "Is everyone participating?" and "Is there anyone I need to make a special effort to follow up with?"

3. Take note of the Supplies list, and the activity in "Digging Into Scripture." In order to ensure that subgroups can complete this task, give them complete newspapers. Take a few minutes before the session to review the newspapers on your own to make sure there will be examples of each type of story for each subgroup. As subgroups will break into halves, you may want to suggest that the half looking for stories illustrating how good people can be gets the obituary or human-interest section. If your group is small, have the entire group separate into two halves where the instructions call for it.

## Session 8 Leader Notes

1. Since this is your group's last session in this book, make sure you have a plan for next week...and beyond.

2. As part of this last session, you may want to consider having people share, either during the "Taste and See" section or at the end of your session, what this study or group has meant to them. This can also be incorporated into the beginning of your prayer time, if you like.

3. Look over the Supplies list and the activity in "Digging Into Scripture." Be sure to provide a variety of seed packets—include both flower and vegetable seeds—so everyone in the group has a different one.

4. Here's one suggestion for making the closing prayer time for this last session special: Have the group form a prayer circle. Then have each person or couple, if comfortable doing so, take a turn standing or kneeling in the middle of the circle while the group prays specifically for them. Your Prayer Coordinator is a good candidate to lead this.

5. Another prayer suggestion: Have group members open and extend their hands as they pray and literally "hand" their concerns to God. Then they should draw their hands in as they "receive" from God in prayer.

# ROLE DESCRIPTIONS

Review the group roles that follow.

We have provided multiple roles to encourage maximum participation. At minimum, there are three roles that we recommend be filled for every session: Leader, Food Coordinator, and Host. These particular roles can also be rotated around the group, if you like. Other roles (Outreach and Inreach Coordinators especially) are best handled by only one person per role, as they involve tasks that may take more than one week to accomplish. It's *your* group—you decide what works best. What's most important is that you work together in deciding.

Not everyone will want to take on a role, so no pressure. But as you come to own a role in your group, you'll feel more connected. You'll even become more comfortable with that role that you're not so sure you want to volunteer for right now.

Read through the following roles together, and write in each volunteer's name after his or her role in your book, so everyone remembers who's who (and what roles may still be available):

## LEADER _____.

Your session Leader will facilitate each session, keeping discussions and activities on track. If a role hasn't yet been filled or the person who normally has a certain role misses a session, the session Leader will also make sure that all tasks and supplies are covered.

## FOOD COORDINATOR _____.

The Food Coordinator will oversee the snacks for each group meeting. This role not only builds the fellowship of the group, but it is an especially important role for this particular study, since specific snacks are assigned for each session and are used to lead group members into the meaning of each session.

**HOST** _____.

Your Host will open up his or her home—and help group members and visitors feel *at* home. It sounds simple enough, but the gift of hospitality is critical to your group. If group members don't feel welcome, chances are they won't stay group members for long. Your Host should also be responsible for supplying—or locating someone who *can* supply—the items in the Supplies list at the beginning of each session. (They're usually common household items, so don't panic.)

**OUTREACH COORDINATOR** _____.

Different sessions often highlight different ways to reach out—sharing the Word, extending personal invitations to others to come to your group, or participating in service projects where your group meets the needs of those in your neighborhood or community. Your Outreach Coordinator will champion and coordinate those efforts to reach outside of your group.

**GROUP CARE ("INREACH") COORDINATOR** _____
_____. Everyone needs a pat on the back once in a while. Therefore, every group also needs a good Inreach Coordinator—someone who oversees caring for the personal needs of group members. That might involve coordinating meals for group members who are sick, making contact with those who have missed a session, arranging for birthday/anniversary celebrations for group members, or sending "just thinking of you" notes.

**PRAYER COORDINATOR** _____.

Your Prayer Coordinator will record and circulate prayer requests to the rest of the group during the week, as well as channel any urgent prayer requests to the group (that may come up during the week). He or she may also be asked to lead the group in prayer at the close of a session.

## SUBGROUP LEADER(S) _____

_____.

To maximize participation, and also to have enough time to work through the session, at various points we recommend breaking into smaller subgroups of three or four persons. Therefore, you'll need Subgroup Leaders. This is also a great opportunity to develop leaders within the group (who may potentially like to lead new groups in the future).

## CHILD CARE COORDINATOR _____.

Your Child Care Coordinator will make arrangements to ensure that children are cared for while their parents meet, either at the Host's home or at some other agreed-upon location(s). Depending on the makeup of your group, this could be a make-or-break role in ensuring you have a healthy group.

Again, if you don't have volunteers for every role (aside from Leader, Food Coordinator, and Host), that's OK. You may need to think about it first or become more comfortable before making a commitment. What's important is that once you commit to a role, you keep that commitment. If you know you'll miss a session, give the session Leader as much advance notice as possible so your role can be covered.

Whether you volunteer for a role now or want to think things over, take time before the next session to look over the "Group Role Tips" section that begins on the following page. You'll find plenty of useful ideas that will help your group and your role in it (or the role you're considering) be the best they can be.

# GROUP ROLE TIPS

## FOOD COORDINATOR

1. Sometimes your snack will be a surprise to the rest of the group. Be sure to work closely with your Host and Leader so that the timing of your snacks helps this session be the best it can be.

2. You may need to arrive early to set up the surprise. Be sure to discuss your arrival time with the Host.

## FOOD COORDINATOR ASSIGNMENTS AND IDEAS

### Session 1

For this session, provide two sets of bowls of ice cream. (Paper bowls are fine to use for this snack, especially as you'll need to provide two sets for the entire group within a fairly brief period of time.)

The first set of bowls—one for each member of the group—should be regular, if not quality, ice cream (i.e., "the good stuff"). The second set of bowls should be of some kind of substitute ice cream (low-fat, low-sugar, or something similar that doesn't quite taste like "real" ice cream). If certain members of your group are lactose-intolerant, serve them cups of regular and diet soda instead.

Keep the two sets of ice cream separated, so group members will grab from the "real" group first. You could serve each group of bowls yourself, if you like.

### Session 2

For this session you'll need:

• 3 or 4 assorted boxes of cereal, at least one per subgroup

• enough milk for everyone to enjoy some cereal

Also make sure there's enough bowls and spoons for everyone in the group, because they'll also be used later in the session.

## Session 3

For this session, provide a variety of chocolates: dark chocolate, milk chocolate, filled chocolates, and any other varieties you'd like. Don't cut back on the quality—make this snack special. If finances are an issue, provide fewer chocolates rather than providing chocolates of lower quality. The specific type or amount of chocolate you provide isn't as important as the experience of eating it. (And your group will appreciate you providing that experience!)

## Session 4

Tonight's suggested snack is fruit-covered cheesecake and coffee. Have some tea available as well, so group members who are concerned about getting to sleep tonight can substitute it for coffee if they feel they need to.

## Session 5

Tonight you'll have two different sets of snacks: chocolate-chip cookies and carrots and dip. Look over the "Taste and See" section to get an idea of how they'll be used. Make sure you have some of both snacks left after your subgroup time to give your "carrot people" a chance to get caught up if they like (and to give your chocolate-chip people a chance to soothe their guilt!). Keep extras hidden if you need to, to make sure you have leftovers.

## Session 6

For this session, serve a selection of the following, all in separate containers:

- cold cuts (you can include cheese here, if you like)
- cake or pie
- pizza (the frozen kind is fine)
- soda
- fruit punch
- coffee or tea

Don't break the bank here, but make sure there's enough food for your group.

### Session 7

Your snack for today is fruit: specifically, apples, oranges, and peaches (or mangoes). It's important to use these fruits because many of us have difficulty knowing how good the fruit is on the inside just by looking at the outside.

### Session 8

Your snack for this last session is a selection of dried fruit and nuts. Be sure to find out ahead of time if anyone has allergies and, if so, make sure problem ingredients aren't mixed with the others (although it's OK to offer them separately).

Thanks again for all your work in making this a successful study!

## HOST

1. Before your group gets together, make sure the environment for your session is just right. Is the temperature in your home or meeting place comfortable? Is there enough lighting? Are there enough chairs for everyone? Can they be arranged in a way to include everyone? Is your bathroom clean and "stocked"? Your home doesn't need to win any awards—just don't let anything be a distraction from your time together.

2. Once your session's started, do what you can to keep it from being interrupted. When possible, don't answer the phone. Ask people to turn off their cell phones or pagers, if necessary. If your phone number's an emergency contact for someone in the group, designate a specific person to answer the phone, so your session can continue to run smoothly.

3. If you're responsible for the supplies for your study, be sure to read through the Supplies list before each session. If there's any difficulty in supplying any of the materials, let your Leader know or contact someone else in the group who you know has them. The items required for each session are usually common household items, so most weeks this will be pretty easy. Make sure everything's set up before the group arrives.

4. Be sure also to check out what the Food Coordinator has planned each week. Sometimes the snack is a surprise, so he or she may need your help in

*keeping* it a surprise. Your Food Coordinator may also need to arrive a few minutes early to set up, so be sure to work out a time for his or her arrival before the meeting.

5. And, of course, make your guests feel welcome. That's your number-one priority as Host. Greet group members at the door, and make them feel at home from the moment they enter. Spend a few minutes talking with them after your session. Let them know you see them as people and not just "group members." Thank them for coming as they leave.

## OUTREACH COORDINATOR

1. Don't forget: New people are the lifeblood of a group. They will keep things from getting stale and will keep your group outwardly focused—as it should be. Encourage the group to invite others.

2. Don't overlook the power of a personal invitation—even to those who don't know Jesus. Invite people from work or your neighborhood to your group, and encourage other group members to do the same.

3. Take special note of the Touching Your World section at the end of each session. The last "weekly challenge" is often an "outreach" assignment that can be done either individually or as a group. Be sure to encourage and follow up with group members who take on these challenges.

4. If group members choose an outreach option for their weekly challenge, use part of your closing time together to ask God for help in selecting the right service opportunity and that God would bless your group's efforts. Then spend some time afterward discussing what you'll do next.

5. Consider having an event before you begin your BibleSense study (or after you finish it). Give a "no obligation" invite to Christians and non-Christians alike, just to give them an opportunity to meet the others in your group. Do mention what the group will be studying next, so guests have an opportunity to consider joining you for your next study. Speak with your Leader before making any plans, however.

6. As part of your personal prayer time, pray that God would bring new people to the group. Make this a regular part of your group's prayer time as well.

# GROUP CARE ("INREACH") COORDINATOR

1. Make a point of finding out more about your group members each week. You should be doing this as a group member, but in your role as Inreach Coordinator, you'll have additional opportunities to use what you learn to better care for those in your group.

2. If a group member has special needs, be sure to contact him or her during the week. If it's something the group can help with, get permission first and then bring the rest of the group into this ministry opportunity.

3. Find out the special dates in your group members' lives, such as birthdays or anniversaries. Make or bring cards for other group members to sign in advance.

4. If someone in your group is sick, has a baby, or faces some kind of emergency, you may want to coordinate meals for that person with the rest of the group.

# PRAYER COORDINATOR

1. Pray for your group throughout the week, and encourage group members to pray for one another. Keep a prayer list, and try to send out prayer reminders after each session.

2. Be sure to keep your group up to date on any current or earlier prayer requests. Pass on "praise reports" when you have them. Remind them that God not only hears but also *answers* prayer.

3. Remember that the role is called Prayer *Coordinator*, not Official Pray-er for the Group (whether that's what your group would prefer or not). At the same time, some members of your group may be uncomfortable praying aloud. If there are several people in your group who don't mind praying, one person could open your prayer time and another close it, allowing others to add prayers in between. Give everyone who wants to pray the opportunity to do so.

4. Prayers don't have to be complex, and probably shouldn't be. Jesus himself said, "When you pray, don't babble on and on as people of other religions do. They think their prayers are answered merely by repeating their words again and again" (Matthew 6:7).

5. If some group members are intimidated by prayer, begin prayer time by inviting group members to complete a sentence as they pray. For example, ask everyone to finish the following sentence: "Lord, I want to thank you for..."

6. Don't overlook the power of silent prayer, and don't automatically fill dead spaces in your prayer time. God may be trying to do that by speaking into that silence. You might even consider closing a session with a time of silent prayer.

## SUBGROUP LEADER(S)

1. These sessions are designed to require a minimum of preparation. Nonetheless, be sure to read over each session and watch the DVD in advance to get comfortable with those sections where you may be responsible for leading a subgroup discussion. Highlight any questions you think are important for your subgroup to spend time on during next session.

2. Try not to have the first or last word on every question (or even most of them). Give everyone the opportunity to participate. At the same time, don't put anyone on the spot—let subgroup members know they can pass on any question they're not comfortable answering.

3. Keep your subgroup time on track. There are suggested time limits for each section. Encourage good discussion, but don't be afraid to "rope 'em back in." If you do decide to spend extra time on a question or activity, consider skipping or spending less time on a later question or activity so you can stay on schedule.

# CHILD CARE COORDINATOR

There are several ways you can approach the important issue of child care. Discuss as a group which alternative(s) you'll use:

1. The easiest approach may be for group members to make their own child care arrangements. Some might prefer this; others may not be able to afford it on their own. If a parent or couple needs financial assistance, see if someone else in the group can help out in this area.

2. If your meeting area is conducive to it, have people bring their children to the meeting and have on-site child care available so parents can pay on a child-by-child basis.

3. If most or all of your group members have young children, you could also consider rotating child care responsibilities within the group rather than paying someone else.

4. If there are members in your group with older children who are mature enough to watch the younger children, pay them to handle your child care. Maybe they can even do their own lesson. If so, Group offers a number of great materials for children of all ages—go to www.group.com to find out more.

5. Check to see if the youth group at your church would be interested in providing child care as a fundraiser.

> It is wise to pre-screen any potential child care worker—paid or volunteer—who is watching children as part of a church-sanctioned activity (including a home Bible study). Your church may already have a screening process in place that can be utilized for your group. If not, Group's Church Volunteer Central network (www.churchvolunteercentral.com) is a great resource, containing ready-made background-check and parental-consent forms, as well as articles and other online resources.